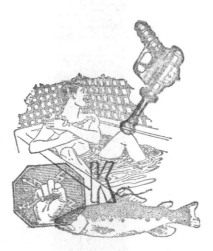

A. Activism; iii. Legal/Politics

HOMOSEXUALS
AND
THE MILITARY

Previous Books by the Institute for Sex Research

SEXUAL BEHAVIOR IN THE HUMAN MALE (1948)
Alfred C. Kinsey, Wardell B. Pomeroy, and Clyde E. Martin

SEXUAL BEHAVIOR IN THE HUMAN FEMALE (1953)
Alfred C. Kinsey, Wardell B. Pomeroy, Clyde E. Martin,
and Paul H. Gebhard

PREGNANCY, BIRTH AND ABORTION (1958)
Paul H. Gebhard, Wardell B. Pomeroy, Clyde E. Martin,
and Cornelia V. Christenson

SEX OFFENDERS (1965)
Paul H. Gebhard, John H. Gagnon, Wardell B. Pomeroy, and
Cornelia V. Christenson

HOMOSEXUALS AND THE MILITARY

A Study of Less Than Honorable Discharge

COLIN J. WILLIAMS
AND
MARTIN S. WEINBERG

1817

HARPER & ROW, PUBLISHERS
New York, Evanston, San Francisco, London

FIRST EDITION

STANDARD BOOK NUMBER: 06-0146648

LIBRARY OF CONGRESS CATALOG CARD NUMBER: 71-138772

CONTENTS

FOREWORD

In the Task Force Report on Homosexuality requested by the Director, Dr. Stanley Yolles, for the National Institute of Mental Health, an interdisciplinary panel of social and behavioral scientists, jurists, and theologians recommended that research was urgently needed on the effects of current social policy concerning homosexuals. It expressed the judgment, in the light of available evidence, that this policy does more social harm than good. This book is an excellent illustration of the validity of that judgment concerning one form of social policy, that of the military. It is to be hoped that it will come to the attention of military policy makers, as well as the general public and researchers in the social and behavioral sciences. It merits a large audience not only because of its theoretical excellence but also because of its implications for social policy and continued research on homosexuality and other forms of social deviance.

The experimental design of the research involves the comparison of a group of homosexual men who received an Honorable Discharge from the armed services with a comparable group who received a less than honorable discharge. It is unfortunate, as the authors point out, that both groups were members of homosexual organizations and were therefore atypical in some respects of the larger homosexual population. However, the findings from another study conducted in Chicago in which only 20 percent were members of a homosexual organization tend to confirm the validity of the findings in the present study.

The theoretical basis of the research will be of great interest to all social scientists working in the area of social deviance because of the dominance of the labeling approach in current sociological theory. The theoretical presentation of labeling "theory" is excellent, the best I have read. I am in complete agreement with

vii

the authors' critique of the labeling approach for its failure to take into account the role of those who engage in deviant acts, and I commend their emphasis on the variables characterizing the potential deviant as well as those involving the labeling agencies. The development of predictions from the perspective both of labeling theory and of Schutz's ideas concerning typification of self and others is highly ingenious and an exemplary model of a research design.

I found the review of policy and attitudes of the armed forces one of the most valuable aspects of the book. The authors' presentation of the official policies of the various branches of the military from 1940 to the present time, as well as the organizational processes in the application of the label "less than honorable" from its initial phases to the final discharge, is excellent. The evidence presented indicates that it is a problem of considerable magnitude. The best estimate from military records is that 2,000 men per year are given a less than honorable discharge for homosexuality. As the authors point out, the interrogation procedures and the threats and promises to the accused are designed to intimidate and terrorize so that he waives his rights to a hearing and thus is almost automatically guaranteed an Undesirable Discharge. The violation of civil rights has seldom been more devastatingly documented. The unjust and immoral policy of the military in its treatment of homosexuals is also illustrated by the evidence that the large majority of those who serve, among whom are many officers, do so with honor and receive Honorable Discharge. It is clear that the inhuman and unjust policy of the military should be fought by all concerned citizens, as well as by homosexuals themselves. It is also clear that the homosexual organizations are rendering a valuable service both in protesting military policy and in informing homosexuals of their rights when interrogated by the military.

From a theoretical and practical viewpoint, one of the most valuable discoveries is the role played by the homosexual in the discovery by the military of his sexual orientation. It substantiates the fact that the *interaction* between the attitudes and behavior of the homosexual and the action of the military results in an Undesirable Discharge. The theoretical implications for labeling theory are clear. From a practical standpoint, those who counsel homosexuals entering the armed services could benefit greatly by an understanding of the ways in which the homosexual contributes to his own Undesirable Discharge.

Although few of the predictions concerning the subjective and objective differences between the two groups were confirmed, the value of the data on many aspects of homosexual life is very great indeed. The two most important differences are that those with less than honorable discharges suffered greater difficulties in securing employment and that they considered and attempted suicide more often. The latter is related to the time of discharge. The finding that these effects of an Undesirable Discharge are traumatic at the time but temporary in character is very surprising and contrary to the authors' predictions. I agree in part that active members of homosexual organizations are actively involved in the homosexual culture and are more likely to accept themselves in a positive way and thus come to terms with the effects of an official labeling. Another explanation, however, is that the majority of both groups were white-collar workers and professional or small businessmen and, therefore, less subject to the traumatic effects of the loss of security clearance which follows an Undesirable Discharge.

This does not mitigate the over-all excellence of this book. It is greatly to be hoped that it will serve as a model for more research on homosexuality and the military, using more representative samples of the homosexual population, in spite of the extraordinary difficulties of obtaining such samples. It is also of the greatest importance that the social implications of this book should be recognized and acted on by the appropriate military agencies.

Evelyn Hooker
Chairman, National
Institute of Mental
Health Task Force
on Homosexuality

PREFACE

In this book a conception of deviance is used to organize a study of male homosexuals less than honorably discharged from the military. We wish to emphasize to the reader that this conception is a purely sociological one. That is:

. . . deviance . . . is defined by what people say and do about persons, situations, acts, or events. For deviance to become a social fact, somebody must perceive an act, person, situation, or event as a departure from social norms, must categorize that perception, must report the perception to others, must get them to accept this definition of the situation, and must obtain a response that conforms to this definition. Unless all these requirements are met, deviance as a social fact does not come into being. . . .[1]

In no way is our use of the term "deviant" to imply any more than this—viz., that persons do set one another off from their fellows in the above manner and that this differentiation has social consequences. Nor is it to imply that we always agree with such social differentiation or that we conceive of the deviance in any other way—e.g., as being psychologically deviant. Our own position with regard to homosexuals and the military is provided in the Epilogue. Our hope is that this book will in some way help to change the more traditional position taken on this subject. Also, the general term "homosexuality" is employed throughout. While the study deals only with *male* homosexuals, this was an editorial decision on the part of the publisher made for the sake of brevity.

We wish to acknowledge our appreciation to the Mattachine

---

[1] Earl Rubington and Martin S. Weinberg, *Deviance: The Interactionist Perspective* (New York: Macmillan, 1968), p. v.

Society of New York and the Society for Individual Rights of San Francisco, who cooperated with us in our research, to the subjects who provided us with the benefit of their experiences, and to the granting agencies that funded the research. The research developed out of a National Institute of Mental Health grant provided for a broader study of homosexuals (MH 13556) and was replicated with data from another National Institute of Mental Health grant (MH 12535). Funds were also provided by the Division of Alcohol Problems and General Welfare of the Methodist Board of Christian Social Concerns and by the Rutgers University Research Council.

C.J.W.

M.S.W.

Bloomington, Indiana

HOMOSEXUALS
AND
THE MILITARY

Chapter 1

THEORETICAL CONSIDERATIONS

Current among sociological conceptions of deviance is an approach which concerns itself less with the attributes of the person or persons said to have violated a social rule than with the character of the reactions of other persons to these attributes and events. This view is inherent in the way the approach conceptualizes the social essence of "deviance"; thus Howard Becker's definition,

. . . deviance is not a quality of the act the person commits, but rather a consequence of the application by others of rules and sanctions to an "offender." The deviant is one to whom that label has successfully been applied; deviant behavior is behavior that people so label.[1]

This perspective, sometimes called the "labeling" approach to deviance, thus views "the deviant" sociologically, as the product of social differentiation processes.[2] The questions that are raised by this approach concern the behaviors that are labeled as deviant, the processes by which the labels are successfully applied or avoided, and the consequences of such processes for both labelers and labeled.

The present study is designed to shed light on one such situation: irregular separation from the military for reasons concerning homosexuality. The particular "label" in question here is the character of discharge given to military personnel—in this case, less than honorable discharge. Both the nature of the label and the formal context of its application will be considered later;

---

[1] Howard S. Becker, *Outsiders: Studies in the Sociology of Deviance* (New York: Free Press, 1964), p. 9.

[2] The approach is sometimes, and more accurately, called the "interactionist" approach to deviant behavior. See Earl Rubington and Martin S. Weinberg, *Deviance: The Interactionist Perspective* (New York: Macmillan, 1968).

1

suffice it here to say that the label is a deviant one in that it constitutes a stigma by intention and implied consequence.[3]

The particular questions posed have been cast in terms of the labeling perspective not only so that we might benefit from previous research utilizing this perspective but also in order to examine some of its central assumptions. We do not wish to suggest that this will be a *test* of labeling "theory," for, at the moment, the approach is more a conception than a theory—that is, there exists no set of testable empirical propositions that constitute "labeling theory."[4]

We shall ask the following questions: (1) What are the social processes that lead to the successful application of the label "less than honorable discharge"? and (2) what are the consequences for those so labeled?

THE SUCCESSFUL APPLICATION OF DEVIANT LABELS

It has been pointed out that a characteristic of the labeling approach is its focus on situations of social ambiguity involving, first, the processes surrounding the perception of whether or not a behavior is deviant and, second, whether an action does in fact violate the norm established.[5] This latter concern is extended to include cases where deviant behavior is attributed to a "condition" of the person involved and where attempts are made to discover the condition.[6]

---

[3] We follow Goffman's use of the term here and throughout. "The term stigma . . . will be used to refer to an attribute that is deeply discrediting. . . ." Erving Goffman, *Stigma: Notes on the Management of Spoiled Identity* (Englewood Cliffs, N.J.: Prentice-Hall, 1965), p. 3.

[4] This distinction between a conception and a theory in regard to the labeling perspective is made by Gibbs. See Jack Gibbs, "Conceptions of Deviant Behavior: The Old and the New," *Pacific Sociological Review,* 9 (Spring 1966), 12.

[5] David Bordua, "Recent Trends: Deviant Behavior and Social Control," *Annals of the American Academy of Political and Social Science,* 369 (January 1967), 150. Bordua refers to the "societal reaction" school, which is identical with the labeling approach, though perhaps a term wider in its implications.

[6] *Ibid.,* p. 151. For one study that examines the patterns of inference involved in imputing a deviant condition, see John I. Kitsuse, "Societal Reactions to Deviant Behavior: Problems of Theory and Method," *Social Problems,* 9 (Winter 1962), 247–56.

The beginning of the interactive process between deviant and labeler most often occurs when a person has broken or is accused of breaking a social rule.[7] The essential precondition to being *sociologically* a deviant is that this be known to others. The end of the process sees him stamped "effectively" with a deviant label which, according to Rubington and Weinberg, means:

. . . simply that the label does in fact make a difference in social relations, not only for the person so labelled but also for the person or persons affixing the label. A new set of interpretations is made available for understanding the person adjudged a deviant. And when these interpretations take effect, a person has been socially reconstituted.[8]

Now the mere fact of labeling a person as deviant is not sufficient to produce a social deviant; this depends largely on what social characteristics typify the labeler and the labeled. This is so because sustaining the judgment that a person is deviant requires the validation of others, and this validation is more forthcoming the higher the rank of the labeler or the greater his expertise. Social validation, therefore, is a matter of differential power in most cases. This does not mean, of course, that we ignore the more informal processes of validation, such as rumor.

The greatest power to apply labels is in the hands of formal agencies of social control, such as the police and the courts, which are backed up in their operations by the power of the state. A great deal of attention has been paid to the operations of social control agencies by sociologists who employ the labeling perspective, especially the stereotypes or categories they use in defining who is deviant and how such deviants should be processed.[9] It is not our intention to closely examine the methods by

---

[7] To become a social deviant it is not necessary to have in fact broken a rule. See Becker's discussion of the falsely accused, Becker, *op. cit.*, pp. 20ff. Conversely, breaking a rule in itself is not sufficient to produce a social deviant. See Becker's discussion of secret deviance, *op. cit.*

[8] Rubington and Weinberg, *op. cit.*, p. 9.

[9] See Thomas J. Scheff, "The Societal Reaction to Deviance: Ascriptive Elements in the Psychiatric Screening of Mental Patients in a Midwestern State," *Social Problems,* 11 (Spring 1964), 401–13; David Sudnow, "Normal Crimes: Sociological Features of the Penal Code in a Public Defender's Office," *Social Problems,* 12 (Winter 1965), 255–

which the military selects out and processes its deviants, although that would make a fascinating study; we shall, however, note certain patterns as suggested to us by official military rulings and the experiences of the respondents themselves.

The attention paid to social control agencies has been in accord with their importance in modern society and with the theoretical bias of the investigators. Most of the findings have documented the discrepancies between formal statements of procedures and actual operations and the immense power of social control agencies in the social production of deviants.[10]

This emphasis on labelers, rather than attributes of deviants, has been rich in its contribution to a better understanding of deviance as a social fact. However, a case can be and has been made that the reaction to older conceptions of deviance has been an overreaction and that valuable truths in these earlier perspectives have been ignored. Bordua makes the following comment about labeling theory's conception of the deviant:

. . . it assumes an essentially empty organism or at least one with little or no autonomous capacity to determine conduct. The process of developing deviance seems all societal response and no deviant stimulus.[11]

This is perhaps an overreaction to an overreaction. Becker, for example, does spell out a theory of why some people break rules

---

76; William J. Chambliss and John T. Liell, "The Legal Process in the Community Setting," *Crime and Delinquency,* 12 (October 1966), 310–17.

[10] See Edwin M. Schur, *Crimes Without Victims* (Englewood Cliffs, N.J.: Prentice-Hall, 1965) for the role played by legal agencies in the production of "crimes without victims."

[11] Bordua, *op. cit.,* p. 153. A similar point is raised by Gibbs and Lorber: "Why do some persons commit a given act while others do not? . . . the new perspective does not generate an answer to this question." Gibbs, *op. cit.,* p. 12.

"The theoretical bias of the labelling approach has helped form a more purely sociological analysis of deviance and social control. Neglect of the deviant, however, while possibly justified operationally, creates large gaps in the study of deviance." Judith Lorber, "Deviance as Performance: The Case of Illness," *Social Problems,* 14 (Winter 1967), 302.

and some do not in terms of what he calls "commitment,"[12] and for other labeling theorists, attributes of the deviant himself are not entirely irrelevant. The point is well taken, however; for example, in some of Goffman's writings on mental patients his use of the concept "career contingencies" appears to treat the mental patient as a pawn, subject to the vagaries of all kinds of situational exigencies.[13] The truth, of course, is that neither emphasis is more "correct" than the other—self and other variables interact in the production of deviants, and particular theoretical stances direct the researchers more to one focus than another.

In this study we were aware of the possible discrepancy between official and actual procedures that characterize the operation of the military organization; since we were not able to study these operations directly, we therefore must be careful in making statements on the role of the "other" in the application of the deviant label. What we did study were those persons who were identified and labeled as deviant by the military organization. It will be our first task to ask what role *they* play in the interaction sequence that eventually terminates in their being assigned a deviant status. Operationally the question can be posed as follows: In a comparison of homosexuals who have been discharged under less than honorable conditions from the military with those who received honorable discharges, what factors distinguish the former from the latter with regard to their being selected and identified as deviant by military authorities?

A satisfactory answer to this question will allow us to consider the process of "being discovered." Labeling theory has been viewed as taking the side of the "underdog" in that the deviant is seen as a victim of the somewhat arbitrary procedures of control

---

[12] Becker, *op. cit.*, pp. 25ff.
[13] See Erving Goffman, "The Moral Career of the Mental Patient," in Goffman (ed.), *Asylums: Essays on the Social Situation of Mental Patients and Other Inmates* (Garden City, N.Y.: Doubleday, Anchor Books, 1961), pp. 125–69. For example, p. 135: ". . . mental patients distinctively suffer not from mental illness, but from contingencies."

agencies.[14] He is more "sinned against than sinning," as it is a matter of chance or racial or socioeconomic factors that decide whether he is selected for a deviant role, rather than any behavior on his part. This may or may not be the case; the evidence is equivocal.[15] What we wish to do in the present research is to examine in one particular situation what the effects of the deviant's behavior are on the application of the label. What is the contribution made by the deviant himself to his discovery; to what extent is he an active participant in the process?

Thus, we shall conceptualize the process of labeling as involving two sets of variables: (1) those characterizing the labelers themselves and including their particular commonsense theories of deviance, their sets of typifications or diagnostic categories,[16] the nature of their mandate, the extent of their surveillance activities, and the manner in which they process rule breakers that come under their auspices; (2) those characterizing the potential deviant. Here we are given less guidance by labeling theory, except that generally his rank and power are important concerns, as, of course, is his race. Another set of factors we propose here are those that are more under the deviant's own control and which place him more or less "at risk" with respect to the scanning operations of control agencies. These will include the extent and type of his deviance, his *modus operandi* and general competence in performing deviant acts, and whether he has support to sustain a deviant role and protect himself from social and psychological punishments.

Both these sets of variables will, of course, interact in the production of social deviants, but as we have mentioned, we are

---

[14] For the most articulate of these criticisms, see Alvin W. Gouldner, "The Sociologist as Partisan: Sociology and the Welfare State," *American Sociologist*, 3 (May 1968), 103–16.

[15] See Bordua's review of the evidence as concerns the police and juveniles. Bordua, *op. cit.*, pp. 155ff.

[16] For a general discussion of typifications and diagnostic categories employed by social control agencies, see Thomas J. Scheff, "Typification in the Diagnostic Practices of Rehabilitation Agencies," in *Sociology and Rehabilitation*, Marvin B. Sussman, ed. (Cleveland: American Sociological Association, 1966), pp. 139–47.

more concerned in this research with the latter set. With regard to this, we conceptualized the following variables as being the most important in determining which homosexuals came to the attention of military authorities.

BEING DISCOVERED

Two variables expected to be important were, first, sexual habits before entering the military and, second, the manner in which homosexual satisfaction was obtained during the period of military service.

HOMOSEXUAL FREQUENCY PRIOR TO INDUCTION INTO THE MILITARY

If a person had frequently engaged in homosexual behavior before he entered the military, then it is reasonable to expect that he will perceive and evaluate the military situation in terms of the opportunities open to a homosexual to a greater degree than do those persons whose homosexual behavior had been less frequent prior to their induction. For this reason we expected discovery to be positively related to frequency of homosexual sex before induction.

THE NATURE OF HOMOSEXUAL CONDUCT WHILE IN THE MILITARY

The way in which the homosexual manages his sex in the military was expected to be related to discovery. We anticipated a positive relationship between discovery and (a) frequency of homosexual sex while in service and (b) the degree to which such sex is engaged in with other military personnel. Those homosexuals who frequently engage in sex while in the military place themselves more at risk than those who have little sex. Having other servicemen as partners also increases the risk of discovery. (For example, in prosecuting cases, military authorities endeavor to find out the names of all partners of the accused who are also servicemen; this is often done by threats and promises to the accused, or through the inspection of personal effects—letters, diaries, and the like.)

The manner in which a homosexual is discovered is also of interest. It is our contention, which we examine later, that manner of discovery is closely associated with the variables that determine discovery in the first place.

THE CONSEQUENCES OF BEING LABELED DEVIANT

For those persons effectively labeled as deviant, consequences can range from a short, sharp shock whereby the individual resolves never to break rules again, to continuous systematic deviance as a way of life.[17] Effects will, of course, vary with such things as the seriousness of the rule broken, the nature and extent of the societal reaction to this, and the deviant's own attempts at managing the situation. The process, therefore, as in the case of becoming labeled, will involve the interaction of labelers and labeled. It has been conceptualized in the following way.[18]

There is first a change in the individual's public identity whereby new interpretations are made about the kind of person he is. Rather than being viewed in terms of his old statuses and roles, he is placed in new roles and statuses. He no longer is the person that everyone took him to be but someone capable of breaking rules; therefore trust is withdrawn from him. Now it is assumed that not only may he commit the same act again but also that he possesses other undesirable attributes and is capable of committing other deviant acts.[19] Using Hughes' notion of "master status" (those statuses which override all others), Becker says that the status of deviant is a master status; people react to this status before others that the person may occupy which re-

---

[17] Systematic deviance is a concept introduced by Lemert. "Systematic deviation appears as a subculture or as a behavior system, accompanied by special social organization and formalized status, roles, morals, and morale distinct from the larger culture." Edwin M. Lemert, *Social Pathology* (New York: McGraw-Hill, 1951), p. 44.

[18] The following account is based on Rubington and Weinberg, *op. cit.*, passim, and Becker, *op. cit.*, pp. 32ff.

[19] Goffman, speaking of the stigmatized, says: "We tend to impute a wide range of imperfections on the basis of the original one . . ." Goffman, *Stigma*, p. 5.

sults in his being treated as though "he were generally rather than specifically deviant."[20]

Being assigned this new role and public identity affects his "life chances." He finds that he no longer has the options available to him that he had before, that losing reputation excludes him from legitimate enterprise, and that his actions are open to new interpretations of an adverse type.

There may finally come into play the self-fulfilling prophecy whereby he may come to satisfy the expectations other people have of him and play the role to which he has been assigned. Thus in Lemert's term his deviation becomes "secondary":

> When a person begins to employ his deviant behavior or a role based upon it as a means of defense, attack, or adjustment to the overt and covert problems created by the consequent societal reaction to him, his deviation is secondary.[21]

This process is by no means inevitable, nor does the individual have to go through each stage in an ordered sequence. Becoming a secondary deviant is only one possible adaptation he may make; it is sometimes the case that his personal identity (what he thinks of himself) and his social identity (what others think of him) do not become consonant.[22]

In re-establishing a satisfactory identity there seem to be two major methods employed by the deviant.[23] First, in cases where one's deviance is hard to keep secret or where the person is committed to his deviant behavior, there will be little attempt at duplicity or presenting a social identity that is false. Instead, the person's resources will be directed toward managing tensions that arise in social interactions with "normals." Often he accepts his deviant role as part of his self and seeks to live with it; this can involve what Lemert calls the positive side of a negative

---

[20] Becker, *op. cit.*, p. 34.
[21] Lemert, *Social Pathology*, p. 76.
[22] For a discussion of personal and social identity, see Rubington and Weinberg, *op. cit.*, pp. 317ff.
[23] These alternatives are discussed at length by Goffman, *Stigma*, pp. 41ff.

identity whereby persons find more satisfactory solutions to their problems through deviant rather than nondeviant behavior.[24] It is not the deviant role that the individual wishes to avoid but, rather, the punishment associated with the role behavior. For those whose deviance cannot be easily hidden, yet who do not wish a deviant role, the situation is, of course, different. For them, identity is based usually on avoiding or denying their deviance.[25]

The second alternative is based upon duplicity, and involves "the management of undisclosed discrediting information about self . . . in brief, passing."[26] Here the individual has a secret differentness that he wishes to hide regardless of whether he continues in his deviance or not. He thus establishes a social identity at variance with his personal identity.[27]

It is more common, however, for the deviant to aspire to the best of both worlds—to carry on his deviance in secret and yet occupy conventional roles and statuses. He, therefore, passes, and does so by means of "information control."[28] The threat of disclosure is always present, yet the stakes are often high enough to make this mode of adjustment a common one for many deviants.

It should be noted here that although the most important catalyst of a deviant career is discovery, as the discussion above indicates, this is not necessary for an individual to build a deviant *personal* identity. It is a *necessary* requirement, however, if we are to speak of an individual possessing a deviant *social* identity. In regard to even this, however, it must again be emphasized that the fact of being discovered is not a *sufficient*

---

[24] Edwin M. Lemert, *Human Deviance: Social Problems and Social Control* (Englewood Cliffs, N.J.: Prentice-Hall, 1967), p. 48.

[25] An empirical study which examines ways in which deviants use passing, avoidance, and denial is Edgerton's study of the mentally retarded. See Robert B. Edgerton, *The Cloak of Competence: Stigma in the Lives of the Mentally Retarded* (Berkeley and Los Angeles: University of California Press, 1967).

[26] Goffman, *Stigma, op. cit.*, p. 42.

[27] Rubington and Weinberg, *op. cit.*, p. 319.

[28] For various types of information control used by deviants, see Goffman, *Stigma,* pp. 91ff.

requirement for establishing a deviant social identity. Moreover, the process from discovery to systematic secondary deviation involves other conditions as well; in fact, it has been argued that the effect of getting caught is more likely to be social control than secondary deviation, and that labeling theory has a "strong tendency to look only at the visible end of the . . . process, that is, at those cases where the societal reaction seems to be involved in the development of stabilized 'career' deviance."[29]

Because of the design of this study, unfortunately, we have no effective means to discover the differential effects of social labelings insofar as this includes those whose careers are deterred. We should like to discuss more specifically the other possible effects of being officially labeled deviant. We divide these effects into two main types. The first we call subjective effects, which refer to the way in which the deviant thinks about himself and his situation, the way he now interprets the social world around him from the vantage point of his new status. In examining this, we are in agreement with the following remarks made by Scott and Lyman:

> Sociologists studying deviant behavior are increasingly thinking about labelled deviants, but few are studying what labelled deviants are thinking.
>
> It has proved fruitful to ask, who gets labelled and what are the fateful consequences for those so labelled. But, in pursuing this question, recent investigators have neglected the qualities of consciousness of the deviants themselves.[30]

---

[29] Bordua, *op. cit.*, p. 153. Empirical evidence for the deterrent effect of punishment is found in Glaser's study of federal prisoners who mentioned the unpleasantness of imprisonment as being the most important factor in making them "go straight," and Bonjean and McGee's study of college students and cheating whereby perceptions of punishment which would be incurred was a major deterrent to cheating. See Daniel Glaser, *The Effectiveness of a Prison and Parole System* (Indianapolis: Bobbs-Merrill, 1964), p. 481; and Charles M. Bonjean and Reece McGee, "Scholastic Dishonesty Among Undergraduates in Differing Systems of Control," *Sociology of Education,* 38 (Winter 1965), 127–37.

[30] Marvin B. Scott and Stanford M. Lyman, "Paranoia, Homosexuality and Game Theory," *Journal of Health and Social Behavior,* 9 (September 1968), 179.

It is our intention to investigate the peculiar "qualities of consciousness" that characterize those who have been singled out as
possessing an undesirable blemish about which "something
should be done."

The next type of effect we call objective effects, which refer to
the objective consequences of being labeled deviant, how the
deviant acts or behaves, or what happens to him, rather than how
he feels. Some of these consequences flow from the deviant himself as a result of interpreting himself and his social situation in a
new light. Other consequences flow from the reaction of other
people toward him and are determined by their interpretation
and evaluation of his particular deviance. Under objective consequences, therefore, we look at the way in which the deviant
relates to conventional social institutions and the extent to which
he is integrated into the larger society.

THE SUBJECTIVE EFFECTS OF BEING LABELED DEVIANT

In attempting to answer the question of how a person evalu-
ates himself and others after being labeled deviant, we are
guided by Alfred Schutz's theory of how people generally con-
struct their subjective worlds.[31]

Answering the question of how men organize their experiences,
Schutz claimed that all men experience the world in the mode of
typicality. By this he meant that both natural and social objects,
events, and relationships are seldom experienced as unique, but
are unique "only within a horizon of typical familiarity and pre-
acquaintanceship."[32] Thus a person's "taken-for-granted" world
consists of a set of "typifications," which act as a scheme of
interpretation for the actor whereby he can locate himself in and
direct himself within the world. This is so because it is presup-
posed of any typicality that what has been typical in the past will
be typical in the future. As Schutz states it,

---

[31] Alfred Schutz, *Collected Papers: I: The Problem of Social Reality*, ed.
Maurice Natenson (The Hague: Martinus Nijhoff, 1962), and *Collected
Papers: II: Studies in Social Theory*, ed. Arvid Brodersen (The Hague:
Martinus Nijhoff, 1964).
[32] Schutz, Vol. I, *op. cit.*, p. 59.

. . . what has been grasped once in its typicality carries along with it a horizon of possible experiences with corresponding references to familiarity, that is, a series of typical characteristics still not actually experienced but expected to be potentially experienced.[33]

It is our system of typifications, therefore, that organizes what Schutz calls our "stock of knowledge" about the world. But what determines what is typed? This is what Schutz calls our "system of relevances" or practical or theoretical "problems at hand."

The reference of the type to the problem for whose solution it has been formed, its problem-relevance as we shall call it, constitutes the meaning of the typification. Thus a series of types of concrete unique objects can be formed, each emphasizing certain aspects which the object has in common with other objects because these aspects alone are relevant to the practical or theoretical problems at hand. Each problem requires thus, another kind of typification.[34]

It is the system of relevance that determines the system of types under which our stock of knowledge is organized.[35]

Our task, therefore, in determining the subjective constitution of a person's social world is to explain his system of relevances, and thus the way he typifies his experiences.

We shall begin by assuming that a person's system of relevances can be grouped under two broad headings: those which concern himself—"Self-Typification"—and those which concern others—"Typification of Others." We now suggest some of the ways in which the officially labeled deviant may typify his world, the deviant in this case being the homosexual less than honorably discharged from the military.

SELF-TYPIFICATION

Self-acceptance. One of the most important consequences of being labeled deviant is that a change may occur in the individual's public identity. As we have previously stated, this change involves other people taking his identity as a deviant as

---

[33] *Ibid.*, p. 282.
[34] Schutz, Vol. II, *op. cit.*, p. 235.
[35] *Ibid.*, p. 257.

his paramount identity over and above all others he may possess. Thus he finds himself typified by others as untrustworthy, immoral, dangerous, or by one or more of many epithets which denote that he is undesirable. Such appraisals on the part of others affect the way in which he thinks and feels about himself.[36] Thus, in general, we would expect that deviants would be less self-accepting than nondeviants, and this even to be the case despite support for a deviant identity that might come from involvement in a subculture of similar deviants. Furthermore, we would expect that problems of self-acceptance are greater for the officially labeled deviant than for those whose deviance has not been brought to the attention of unsympathetic others. The former has had to confront his deviance publicly; he has had his differentness forcibly drawn to his attention and has received sanctions because of it. On the other hand, the secret deviant, though probably aware of public condemnation of his activities, has not experienced such a degrading confrontation. Thus we would expect that the officially labeled homosexual (in the present case, those who received less than honorable discharges from the military) is less self-accepting than the homosexual who had not undergone such a labeling experience.

Self as determined. The deviant is not a passive member in the labeling process. Despite difficulties that arise in achieving an acceptable self, he nonetheless attempts to retain some pride in self against the condemnation of society. One way in which he does this is by seeking justifications for his behavior; such justifications have been called "techniques of neutralization," an important one being "denial of responsibility."[37]

What sometimes occurs is that the deviant sees himself as determined, as not being responsible for his behavior because he

---

[36] This of course refers to the well-known "looking glass" process as proposed by Cooley. See Charles H. Cooley, *Human Nature and the Social Order* (New York: Scribner, 1902).

[37] Gresham M. Sykes and David Matza, "Techniques of Neutralization: A Theory of Delinquency," *American Sociological Review*, 22 (December 1957), 664–70.

is unable to change himself or his behavior. Thus, in general, homosexuals often claim that it is not their "fault" that their sexual proclivities are directed toward members of the same sex; that they were "born that way" or that things could not have turned out differently. This will often be generalized into a pessimistic view of the various "treatments" that the heterosexual world proposes for the homosexual. Again we expect that the officially labeled homosexual makes more use of this justification than those not so labeled. This follows (a) from the expectation that he has more serious problems of self-acceptance, and (b) that he probably has had more occasions when he has been asked to account for his deviance.

Self as normal. The most serious problem faced by the labeled deviant, as we have mentioned, is that his deviance becomes the basis upon which other people build their identification of him. Thus, no matter what other identities he may claim for himself or what valued social attributes he may possess, his deviant identity is the one that becomes paramount in social situations. One response to this on the part of the deviant is to claim that, apart from his deviance, he is no different from others of the same social background. We propose that homosexuals who have been discharged from the military under less than honorable conditions are less likely to feel this way. Their sexuality was the relevant issue in their separation. Regardless of the previous character of their service or of what valued military attributes they possess, they were defined as undesirable and unwanted by the military. We would expect, therefore, that as a result they would be more likely to typify themselves as "abnormal" than homosexuals whose sexual orientation has not been the major basis for a degrading change in status.

Self as a practical methodologist. Another important typification of self is that which, after Garfinkel, we call "self-as-practical-methodologist." Considering a case of an "intersexed" person, he says that her experiences resulted in the following:

Her studies armed her with knowledge of how the organized features of ordinary settings are used by members as procedures for making appearances-of-sexuality-as-usual desirable as a matter of course.[38]

[She] was self consciously equipped to teach normals how normals make sexuality happen in commonplace settings as an obvious, familiar, recognizable, natural, and serious matter of fact.[39]

By this we refer to the uncommonsense knowledge of social structures that Goffman says is one of the secondary gains of stigmatized persons.[40] That is, even though he assumes a determinism in the moves he makes, the officially labeled homosexual does see certain gamelike features of the social world. He sees the rules, and how things taken for granted are no more than cultural events, having the status of mere convention.

Through his own experiences, therefore, the officially labeled homosexual has been a participant in a social process which enforces a certain standard of sexual morality. As victim, we expect that he has become even more aware of how morality is made to "happen" than have those homosexuals not officially labeled.

Sense of exposure. Most deviants do not like to have their deviance exposed. Even those who flaunt their differences (for example, the effeminate, "swishy" homosexual) do so usually in situations over which they have some control. It is the unexpected disclosure of one's deviance, therefore, that is particularly threatening, even though the end result may be only a case of embarrassment for one or both parties concerned. This often leads to the feeling of vulnerability, that "everybody knows" about one's secret failing. The deviant sometimes feels that he is living a lie and that at any moment the identity that he proffers could be exposed as false.

---

[38] Harold Garfinkel, "Passing and the Managed Achievement of Sex Status in an Intersexed Person," in *Studies in Ethnomethodology* (Englewood Cliffs, N.J.: Prentice-Hall, 1967), p. 180.

[39] *Ibid.*, p. 180.

[40] Goffman, *Stigma, op. cit.*, p. 11.

Though this sense of exposure is more or less characteristic of most deviants, we feel that it is more common to the officially labeled deviant. Not only has he been exposed before, but also his deviance often becomes a matter of public record that can catch up with him and discredit whatever front he might be putting forward at the moment. We would expect, therefore, that this feeling of vulnerability would typify more the way the less than honorably discharged homosexual would think about himself than the homosexual who had not undergone such a labeling experience.

TYPIFICATION OF OTHERS

Reciprocity of perspectives. According to Laing, every person may take two distinguishable forms of acting in an interpersonal system.

Each may act on his own experiences or upon the other person's experiences, and there is no other form of personal action possible within this system. That is to say, as long as we are considering personal action of self to self or self to others, the only way one can ever act is on one's own experience or on the other's experience.[41]

The second mode of acting is similar to what Schutz considers when he states that the social world is an intersubjective world. This is so because we attribute to others a "reciprocity of perspectives," the assumption that should we change places with the other, then we would see the world in the same typical way; that is, objects in the world will be common to us both.

Our assumption here is that whereas relationships to nonhomosexual others are extremely relevant to homosexuals, their typification of these others will revolve around their belief that the probability that they assume a "reciprocity of perspectives" with homosexuals will be low. In part, the typification of others is helped by seeing oneself as having uncommon knowledge of social structures—in that just by changing places, without having undergone the same or similar biography, and thus becoming a

---

[41] R. D. Laing, *The Politics of Experience* (London: Penguin Books, 1967), p. 29.

"practical methodologist," reciprocity of perspectives cannot be assumed.

Thus their acts will be based on Laing's first alternative, their own experiences, and will result in the construction of a social world that is uniquely private. But other people cannot be ignored completely. They are incorporated into this unique and individual world, as a particular "them." Laing has described this process in general.

Each person's thinking of what he thinks the other thinks. Each person does not mind a colored lodger, but each person's neighbor does. Each person, however, is a neighbor of his neighbor. What they think is held with conviction. It is indubitable and it is incontestable. The . . . group is a series of others which each serial member repudiates in himself.[42]

His concern with the correct interpretation by heterosexuals of his motives, intentions, and acts lessens. He takes it for granted that his problems are unsharable with others and makes few attempts to find out if this in fact is the case. His constructed social world, therefore, includes a large class of nonhomosexuals who are incapable of understanding him and his problems, who are unsympathetic toward him, and, most of all, who are unfair in their treatment of him. It is the officially labeled homosexual, we feel, who would claim the least reciprocity of perspectives with nonhomosexual others. Unlike the homosexual who has not been so labeled, he suffers through what he feels has been the inability of the heterosexual world to understand his situation. He feels he has been unjustly treated for something that is not his "fault," his sexual orientation, which in addition is a private affair having little relevance for other social situations.

Sense of injustice. This latter point, the sense of injustice, is typical of many deviants, especially those who have become involved with social control agencies of the wider society.[43] We

---

[42] *Ibid.,* pp. 68–69.
[43] An example of this which involves juvenile delinquents is provided by Matza. See David Matza, *Delinquency and Drift* (New York: Wiley, 1964), pp. 101–51.

feel that this typification of others as unjust will especially characterize the homosexual separated from the military with a less
than honorable discharge. Such attitudes will be engendered by a
feeling that the punishment he received does not fit the "crime" he
has committed and by the fact that his identity as deviant is seen
as the most relevant identity he possesses.

In summary, if our analysis is correct, we would predict that,
as compared to those homosexuals who received honorable discharges, those homosexuals who received less than honorable
discharges from the military should be more likely—

1. to be less self-accepting
2. to see themselves as being determined
3. to see themselves as "abnormal"
4. to regard themselves as "practical methodologists"
5. to feel more vulnerable to the exposure of their deviance
6. to assume less reciprocity of perspectives with heterosexuals
7. to feel a sense of injustice toward society

THE OBJECTIVE EFFECTS OF BEING LABELED DEVIANT

The most extreme effects of official labeling have been seen as
secondary deviance and subcultural involvement. Other things
being equal, therefore, we would expect the following objective
consequences of being labeled deviant.

According to Becker,

. . . one tends to be cut off, after being identified as deviant, from
participation in more conventional groups, even though the specific
consequences of the particular deviant activity might never of themselves have caused the isolation had there not been public knowledge
and reaction to it.[44]

. . . the treatment of deviants denies them the ordinary means of
carrying on the routines of everyday life open to most people. Because of this denial, the deviant must of necessity develop illegitimate
routines.[45]

---

[44] Becker, *op. cit.*, p. 34.
[45] *Ibid.*, p. 35.

One result of exclusion from more conventional groups is that the deviant seeks out others who either share or are sympathetic to his deviance. This is especially the case for the officially labeled homosexual who not only looks to other homosexuals to help allay problems of self-esteem but also finds in them a ready source of sexual partners. In addition, if it is true that he feels he cannot extend reciprocity of perspectives to most heterosexuals, then he will further wish to confine his interactions to others who understand the way he feels. The result of this process is that he becomes more confirmed in his deviance.

We would predict, therefore, that as compared to the homosexual who has not undergone such a labeling experience, the homosexual less than honorably discharged from the military is likely to be more frequent, overt, and exclusive in his homosexuality, to be more involved in the homosexual "way of life" or subculture, and to value more the opinions of homosexuals.

We shall be particularly concerned with "knownaboutness." How far is it possible to keep the knowledge that one is deviant a secret? We would expect that the less than honorably discharged homosexual will be more knownabout for two reasons. First, his deviance is a matter of public record which could come to the attention of others that he knows. Second, the fact of having this in his biography can create tensions, the sense of vulnerability we have previously mentioned, so that he might prefer to disclose the facts of his deviance himself rather than have them come to light in a situation over which he has no control.

Despite the fact that we predict that the labeled deviant reduces his participation in conventional groups, it is impossible for him to cut himself off completely from society at large. Thus he will participate in conventional institutions to some degree. Although we do not have the means to examine fully the homosexual's integration into society, we did raise questions about certain of his attachments to selected institutions. In this we were influenced by Simon and Gagnon, who state,

It is necessary to move away from an obsessive concern with the sexuality of the individual, and attempt to see the homosexual in terms of the broader attachments that he must make to live in the world around him. Like the heterosexual, the homosexual must come to terms with the problems that are attendant upon being a member of society.[46]

With regard to the less than honorably discharged homosexual we expected the following:

(a) *Work.* Because of the nature of his discharge, certain occupations are closed to him—for example, jobs in the federal government. In addition, many employers often ask to see a person's discharge papers in addition to or in lieu of other references. Thus, compared to homosexuals who have not been so labeled, we would expect him to have more problems concerning employment.

(b) *Politics.* Increased political participation and political consciousness should characterize the less than honorably discharged homosexuals if what we said about their feeling a "sense of injustice" is correct. We would expect them, more so than homosexuals who have not undergone such a labeling experience, to be interested in changing the system that judged them undesirable. By this we do not mean the military as such but the wider social system which looks down upon the homosexual. Thus their politics are expected to be more radical, and in addition they are expected to be the more active in homophile organizations (groups working for the betterment of the homosexual's social and legal situation).[47]

(c) *Religion.* We decided to include questions on religion, as many of the homosexual's problems are caused by laws and attitudes that are based upon the Judeo-Christian tradition. We felt, therefore, that the less than honorably discharged homosexual would be more likely to reject institutionalized religion than the

---

[46] William Simon and John H. Gagnon, "Homosexuality: The Formulation of a Sociological Perspective," *Journal of Health and Social Behavior,* 8 (September 1967), 181.

[47] We recognize that the opposite would be a viable hypothesis also, that is, that rather than increasing political involvement, the person would be more likely to withdraw from political activity. We have, however, been constructing our hypotheses on the basis of what labeling theorists suggest (which is greater political involvement).

homosexual who has not been so labeled, as he has more directly suffered from policies which, if not based upon, are at least consistent with, conceptions of morality as set forth by many religious practitioners.

Finally, in addition to questions about the homosexual's relation to various institutions, we asked a set of questions which reflected what we called "personal adjustment." According to labeling theory, the social effects of being officially defined as deviant are extremely adverse for many who undergo the experience. Thus it might be expected that these social consequences have psychological effects that are also adverse. For example, the labeled homosexual might show more symptoms of stress after having his transgression forcibly brought home to him than the homosexual whose deviance remains a secret. Questions that referred to such things as anxiety, happiness, the use of drugs and alcohol, and so forth were asked with the expectation that the labeled homosexual would show less personal adjustment. This is not to say that secret deviance does not produce similar psychic costs. Which type of deviant shows less personal adjustment is an empirical question; yet we thought, on balance, that the officially labeled homosexual, because of the traumatic effects of facing his deviance directly, would show more adjustment problems.

In summary, with regard to the objective effects of the labeling experience we expected the following. As compared to homosexuals who left the military with honorable discharges, we expected that those who received less than honorable discharges would be more likely—

1. to engage in frequent, overt, and exclusive homosexuality
2. to be involved in the homosexual "way of life" or subculture
3. to value the opinions of homosexuals more than heterosexuals
4. to be known as homosexual to persons or groups
5. to have experienced problems in the world of work
6. to be politically active (especially in the homophile movement) and politically radical
7. to be less involved with religion

8. to be less psychologically adjusted—for example, show more symptoms reflective of anxiety

We are aware that different hypotheses could be proposed concerning the effects of a deviant label; the more traditional approach to deviant behavior, for example, would have predicted a diminution in rule-breaking as a result of punishment. It is also difficult in some cases to make logical or clear deductions from labeling "theory" as to the effects of labeling. However, it was decided to stick to the perspective as far as possible, *and what its practitioners seem to suggest regarding consequences,* and to see how useful it is in examining one particular example of labeling. Thus what we have termed "hypotheses" should be considered more as orienting ideas used to organize the research rather than propositions deduced from substantive theory.

In this discussion we have said little that is concrete about the military situation, about discharge procedures or, for that matter, about homosexuality. This is by design in that if the labeling perspective purports to be a general perspective, then just by knowing that a person has been officially labeled as deviant, we should expect certain consequences. The results of research using the perspective will, of course, modify its assumptions or at least provide more specific conditions under which various factors operate.[48] It is our hope that the following research, even if in a limited way, may contribute to that end.

Before discussing the methodology employed in the research, the following chapters examine the nature of the deviant label "less than honorable discharge," the way it is applied, and the situation of the homosexual in the military environment.

---

[48] This is a fact that has been noted by Becker, *op. cit.,* p. 36: "Obviously, everyone caught in one deviant act and labelled a deviant does not move inevitably toward greater deviance. . . . The prophecies do not always confirm themselves, the mechanisms do not always work." His discussion of the limiting conditions to increasing deviance is short, however, which reflects the undeveloped nature of the perspective.

Chapter 2

LESS THAN HONORABLE DISCHARGE AS A DEVIANT LABEL: ITS RATIONALE AND APPLICATION

THE ATTITUDE OF THE ARMED FORCES TOWARD HOMOSEXUALITY

It is, and has been for a considerable time, the policy of the armed forces of the United States, to prevent "known" homosexuals or persons suspected of having homosexual tendencies from serving in the military. Prospective draftees during their physical examination must answer the question "Have you ever had or have you now . . . homosexual tendencies?" If a homosexual answers Yes, he is disqualified from serving. If he answers No, he has violated federal law and can be subject to a fine and imprisonment. He is, therefore, in the words of one commentator, "boxed in."[1]

It is also the case that any person engaging in or suspected of homosexual activities or tendencies while in the armed forces is dismissed as soon as possible. The official reasons underlying such attitudes can be seen in the various service policies—for example, those of the Army and the Navy:

It is the policy of the Department of the Army that homosexual personnel will not be permitted to serve in the Army in any capacity; prompt separation of homosexuals is mandatory. The army considers homosexuals to be unfit for military service because their presence impairs the morale and discipline of the army, and that homosexuality is a manifestation of a severe personality defect which appreciably limits the ability of such individuals to function effectively in society. No distinction is made between an individual who commits a single act of homosexuality and one who commits several such acts.[2]

[1] David Sanford, "Boxed In," *New Republic*, 154 (May 21, 1966), 8–9.
[2] Department of the Army answer to a question from the Subcommittee on Constitutional Rights of the Senate Committee on the Judiciary,

Homosexuals and other sexual deviates are military liabilities who cannot be tolerated in a military organization. On developing and documenting cases involving homosexual conduct, commanding officers should be keenly aware that homosexuals are security and reliability risks who discredit themselves and the Navy by their homosexual conduct. Their prompt separation from the service is essential. . . . This instruction is not limited in its application to "true," "confirmed," or "way of life" homosexuals. Knowing participation in a homosexual act or strong tendencies toward such acts constitute a sufficient basis for proceeding hereunder. . . .[3]

There are, of course, other reasons than these which find expression in military regulations for the military's attitude. The belief in the existence of homosexual cliques which exercise influence in obtaining special favors and assignments for their members is one which from time to time is mentioned. Another common assumption is that the homosexual preys upon the innocent. A military lawyer explaining service policy writes: "In addition to strong moral and social taboos, sexual perverts are a corrosive influence because they must have partners and often prey on the youthful, naive or greedy."[4]

In writing of the Second World War period, Eli Ginsberg says: "The Army would not expose normal men to possible seduction by homosexuals especially since the latter might be in a position to take advantage of rank."[5]

Homosexuals, therefore, are defined by fiat as being psychologically disturbed and a threat to the morale, morals, and security of the armed forces.

89th Congress, 2nd Session, 1966, p. 921. This subcommittee which began hearings in 1962 under Senator Sam Ervin, Jr. of North Carolina on the whole area of military justice will be a frequent reference point for this section. The 1966 hearings above, plus those of 1962 (same title, 87th Congress, 2nd Session, 1962) will be referred to throughout as the 1962 or 1966 Subcommittee Hearings.

[3] Secretary of the Navy Instruction, SECNAV 1900.9, dated 20th April, 1964.

[4] John A. Everhard, "Problems Involving the Disposition of Homosexuals in the Service," *Air Force Judge Advocate General's Bulletin*, II, No. 6 (1960), p. 20.

[5] Eli Ginsberg et al., *The Ineffective Soldier: Lessons for Management and the Nation* (New York: Columbia University Press, 1959), Vol. II, p. 112.

To the military, then, the label "homosexual" carries with it a set of assumed auxiliary traits that may or may not in fact accompany the sexual proclivity. Furthermore, just the proclivity itself is sufficient for separation whether or not any homosexual acts are committed. This is so interpreted that those who "habitually and knowingly associate themselves with true confirmed homosexuals" and those who have ever engaged in an act of homosexuality are also likely to be separated.[6] As we shall see, it is only recently that persons who fell in this latter category were given the opportunity to receive a discharge under honorable conditions.

DEALING WITH THE HOMOSEXUAL: 1940 TILL THE PRESENT[7]

During World War II, Army enlisted personnel suspected or charged with homosexual attempts or acts came under Section VIII AR 615–360, along with other personnel who were adjudged as having a wide variety of behavioral problems which were subsumed under the general heading of "inaptness or undesirable habits or traits of character." Discharges under Section VIII were usually of the honorable type, except in the case of psychopathic behavior, chronic alcoholism, or "sexual perversion including homosexuality." Here, such persons were given "Discharge without Honor," the well-known "Blue Discharge" (when such cases did not involve court-martial proceedings). It appeared, therefore, as though the homosexual was being singled out for punishment, which was one of the reasons why military psychiatrists attempted to liberalize the policies toward them. Little success was forthcoming, however, because "It was apparently feared that many homosexuals who were well adjusted would seek to be discharged and that others might claim to be homo-

---

6 Such instructions appear in Air Force Regulation AFR 35–66 as reported by Louis Jolyon West and Albert J. Glass, "Sexual Behavior and the Military Law," in Ralph Slovenko (ed.), *Sexual Behavior and the Law* (Springfield, Ill.: Charles C Thomas, 1965), p. 257.

7 This section relies heavily upon West and Glass, *op. cit.*, and William C. Menninger, *Psychiatry in a Troubled World: Yesterday's War and Today's Challenge* (New York: Macmillan, 1948), ch. 16.

sexual for the purpose of getting out of the Army with honorable discharges."[8]

Persistent efforts were eventually rewarded, however, by the publication of War Department Circular No. 85 issued on March 23, 1946. This order made it clear that enlisted personnel who were to be discharged because of homosexual tendencies, yet had not committed any sexual offense while in the service, could be discharged honorably. For officers in this category, it was further provided that they be permitted to resign under honorable conditions.

After 1947 these more liberal policies were reversed with the issuance of a Department of Defense Memorandum dated October 11, 1949. This directive outlined a harsher policy that was to apply uniformly to all branches of the service.

West and Glass suggest that this change in policy was an outcome of concern by Congress that there were homosexuals employed in the federal government, and that homosexuals posed special risks in terms of security.[9] Whatever the cause, the effect on the military was to take more "seriously" the problem of homosexuality. The regulation also was effective in leading to the establishment of three "classes" of homosexuals:

Class I. Servicemen who have committed homosexual offenses involving force, fraud, intimidation, or the seduction of a minor. These cases are usually tried by general court-martial, and if conviction ensues, sentence usually involves imprisonment, fine, and punitive discharge (Dishonorable or Bad Conduct).

Class II. Servicemen who have willfully engaged in, or attempted to perform, homosexual acts which do not fall under the Class I category. Such persons are usually administratively processed and receive an Undesirable Discharge, though theoretically they can receive Honorable or General Discharges. The majority of homosexuals dealt with by the military fall into this class.

---

8 Menninger, *op. cit.*, p. 230.
9 West and Glass, *op. cit.*, p. 256.

Class III. Servicemen who exhibit, profess, or admit homosexual tendencies or associate with known homosexuals. This class also includes those who were homosexual before entering the service. The common feature of this class is that no homosexual acts or offenses have been committed while in the service. Such cases are processed administratively and can receive Honorable Discharges, though most receive either General or Undesirable Discharges.

Officers who fall into Class II or Class III are usually given the opportunity to resign "for the good of the service" to avoid trial by court-martial. This is comparable to an Undesirable Discharge in that it is tendered under other than honorable conditions.

It was not until 1955 that the regulations were modified again in any extensive way. Changes began with an Army review that included the following:[10]

1. More liberal provisions were made for personnel who were not "true" and "confirmed" homosexuals yet became involved in homosexual acts, so they could be retained in service.
2. Class III cases were more clearly defined as overt, confirmed homosexuals who have not engaged in any homosexual acts since entering the service, or individuals whose homosexual tendencies are such that they are unsuitable for military service.

A further revision of regulations issued September 8, 1958, included the mandatory directive that Class III homosexuals be furnished an Honorable or General Discharge based on the character of the service rendered. It was also made possible at this time for Class II cases to receive an Honorable or General Discharge if the individual performed outstanding or heroic service or service over an extended period.

Despite these changes over the period of concern, the attitude of the armed forces has remained fairly constant with regard to

---

[10] Army Regulations AR 635–89, April 15, 1955. These changes are detailed more fully in West and Glass, *op. cit.*, pp. 268–70.

homosexuality. Homosexuals or persons suspected of homosexual tendencies are *persona non grata* and must be immediately expelled, and under provisions that reflect their condition as much as their behavior. The consequences of this attitude have undergone some change, especially the treatment of those individuals defined as Class III homosexuals. Today it is no longer out of the question for a homosexual to receive a General or Honorable Discharge, and in some cases to be retained in the service. In most cases, however, the outcome is consonant with the attitude: the majority of cases are Class II cases, and for them separation with a less than honorable discharge is almost a forgone conclusion.

ORGANIZATIONAL PROCESSES IN THE APPLICATION OF THE LABEL

The sequence of events that follow the case of a serviceman charged with committing homosexual acts or suspected of homosexual tendencies usually proceeds along the following lines.[11]

INITIAL PHASES

A serviceman usually comes to the attention of military authorities by a report from some source that he has participated in or attempted a homosexual act.[12] These sources are various. For example, he can be reported by civil authorities or by some other serviceman. Military psychiatrists or chaplains with whom he discusses homosexuality might report him, or, as is very common, his name may come up in connection with another case. An equally if not more common occurrence is that the individual himself has confessed homosexual acts or, more likely, tendencies. Finally there is the possibility of being caught *in flagrante delicto*, which, however, does not seem to occur with great frequency.

---

11 This discussion has been greatly assisted by a pamphlet published by the Society for Individual Rights, a homophile organization. See *The Armed Services and Homosexuality* (San Francisco: The Society for Individual Rights, no date).

12 Everhard, *op. cit.*, p. 20.

Since homosexual acts are court-martial offenses, if an investigation is begun, the subject is entitled, before interrogation, to his right to remain silent, to be informed that anything he says may be used against him, and to consult with legal counsel if he so requests. According to the charge, he may be tried by court-martial for sodomy under Article 125 of the Uniform Code of Military Justice, lewd acts (Article 134), or attempts to commit such acts (Article 80). If the command decides to initiate administrative discharge proceedings rather than court-martial, he can go before a board of officers where he can testify and present evidence and witnesses. The accused may, however, waive his right to go before such a board and agree to accept an Undesirable Discharge. If the preliminary information against him cannot be substantiated, he will in most cases be cleared.

PREPARING THE CASE

Military authorities must decide: "Is this a homosexual case we have before us and if so what type?" Their decision is based upon the reports of the various service intelligence agencies,[13] military psychiatrists, and evidence from board hearings when held.

(a) Interrogation. Intelligence officers thoroughly interview each suspect, often with interviews taking up to four hours and sometimes lasting over a number of days. They usually search his personal effects for diaries, letters, magazines, etc. They question his service associates, and it has been known for them to question people who know him in his hometown. In addition, promises and threats may be made and the individual persuaded to undergo polygraph tests. All this is directed at obtaining a confession from the suspect.

(b) Psychiatric evaluation. The individual is sent to a military psychiatrist, who judges what type of homosexual he is (what class), whether he is suffering from mental illness of a kind that would require his separation under medical regulations,

---

[13] The Criminal Investigation Division (C.I.D.) of the Army, the Office of Naval Intelligence (O.N.I.) of the Navy, and the Office of Special Investigation (O.S.I.) of the Air Force.

or whether he is feigning homosexuality in order to leave the service.

BOARD APPEARANCE

In a large number of cases the experience up to this point is enough to produce a confession, waive the right to appear before a board of officers, and accept an Undesirable Discharge.

If the accused serviceman desires a hearing, a board is convened. In almost all cases he will be defended by counsel, either civil (which he must pay for himself) or military (provided by the services).

The purpose of the board is to make findings and recommendations to the commander with discharge authority as to whether the serviceman should be separated or retained. Thus it should be noted that the board is an administrative, not a judicial, tribunal. As such, it is not bound by the rigid procedural and evidentiary requirements of judicial proceedings.[14] This has received adverse comment from many lawyers. The following is typical of the charges against such administrative boards:

By stretching the rules of evidence, as proscribed in the regulations, the government is often allowed to present its entire case without calling witnesses. Written statements are many times substituted for the personal appearance of the witness. The burden on the defense is perhaps heaviest in a AFR 35–66 board (discharge of airmen for homosexual activities) where statements of the other individuals, allegedly partners to the homosexual act, are introduced in evidence. The respondent has no opportunity to cross examine them or face his

---

14 Administrative discharges and the conduct of the boards have been subjected to investigation by the Senate Subcommittee on Constitutional Rights. For an overview of the Subcommittee's findings and recommendations see William A. Creech, "Congress Looks to the Serviceman's Rights," *American Bar Association Journal*, 49 (November 1963), 1070–74.

For discussions especially concerned with administrative discharges see Clifford A. Dougherty and Norman B. Lynch, "The Administrative Discharge: Military Justice?" *George Washington Law Review*, 33 (December 1964), 498–528; and Jerome A. Susskind, "Military Administrative Discharge Boards: The Right to Confrontation and Cross Examination," *Michigan State Bar Journal*, 46 (January 1965), 25–32.

accusers and more often than not the others involved have been discharged. Often the statements of law enforcement officials are used as substitutes for their appearance in court. The respondent's position is often hopeless when he cannot face those who give evidence against him and examine them under oath.[15]

As well as being criticized for not providing the right to confront and cross-examine witnesses, boards have been criticized with regard to the right to legal counsel. We mentioned that all services give the right to be represented by counsel. It does not follow, however, that such a person must be a lawyer.[16] A legally qualified counsel is not a necessary part of the right—this depends upon the availability of a lawyer, which is decided by the convening authority. Both of these weaknesses in military justice are still to be rectified; military boards at present do not have subpoena power, and qualified counsels need not be made available. It is obvious, therefore, that the person accused of homosexual acts or tendencies who appears before such boards can expect small help from them in the face of the way they routinely operate and the prejudice against homosexuals in the armed forces.[17]

DISPOSITION

In the case of those who appear before a board, recommendations as to the proper disposition of each convicted person are forwarded to the convening authority for approval. This authority need not accept the recommendation and has the power to convene a new board. In the Coast Guard and Navy especially, the administrative board is little more than a fact-finding body

---

[15] Susskind, *op. cit.*, p. 30.

[16] See the discussion on "Right to Legal Counsel," in Dougherty and Lynch, *op. cit.*, p. 509.

[17] It was also discovered by the Subcommittee that the military services were resorting to administrative discharges as a means of circumventing the Uniform Code of Military Justice 1950 which had provided safeguards to personnel in respect to the conduct of courts-martial. Thus persons were brought under administrative proceedings who normally would have faced a court-martial solely to increase the probability of conviction. See Creech, *op. cit.*, pp. 1070–71.

that assists the commanding officer in making his decision. Furthermore, the Navy permits the issuance of a discharge *less* favorable than that recommended by a board, whereas the Army and Air Force and, recently, the Coast Guard, do not. Thus, despite any protection during board hearings, such proceedings may have been of little use for some servicemen, depending on the attitude of the reviewing authority.

SEPARATION

In most cases both those recommended by a board for discharge and those who agree to accept an Undesirable Discharge and waive appearing before a board are sent to a unit for discharge. It is possible for them to remain with their own unit, either carrying on their previous duties or being assigned special ones, or to be placed in a hospital, depending on circumstances. Before separation, Army personnel receiving Undesirable Discharges are reduced to the lowest rank. All discharges are told they have forfeited any accumulated leave pay, reminded that they have lost most veteran's benefits, and warned that they can expect "to encounter substantial prejudice" in civilian life. Then they are released.

LESS THAN HONORABLE DISCHARGE AS A STIGMA

Bad Conduct and Dishonorable Discharges are defined as punitive discharges by the military. However, insofar as post-service effects are concerned it is claimed by many that any discharge from the services which is other than honorable is likewise punitive.[18]

It is not necessary for our purposes to examine Bad Conduct and Dishonorable Discharges here, as so few homosexuals, by the nature of their offense and its disposition, are likely to receive

---

[18] Dougherty and Lynch, *op. cit.*, p. 516; and Creech, *op. cit.*, p. 1071, "The public generally does not differentiate between an 'other than honorable' discharge imposed by a court-martial and an undesirable discharge—also under other than honorable conditions—issued administratively by the Armed Services."

them.[19] Instead, we shall examine the punitive nature of the General and Undesirable Discharge.

A General Discharge, even though issued under honorable conditions, nonetheless can have adverse effects. Susskind comments: "As a practical matter there can be no doubt that to some extent a stigma attaches to a general discharge and that this may affect the employment opportunities of a serviceman when he enters civilian life."[20]

Consider the following statement made by Dougherty and Lynch:

It may be argued that receiving a general discharge from the armed forces carries no more stigma or hardship than being fired from a civilian job. Just as a person fired from a job may expect to encounter difficulty obtaining other employment, so should the serviceman who is "fired" from the service. The argument fails, however, in the face of the fact that many enterprises in this country depend for their livelihood upon government contract work, for which security clearances are required and "good character" is a must. The ex-serviceman seeking employment in such an enterprise, if he must relate that his separation from the service was not an honorable discharge, will be told "We have to have a photostatic copy of an honorable discharge before we can hire you."[21]

We might expect the situation to be worse as regards an Undesirable Discharge. To begin with, in terms of benefits such as those administered by the Veterans Administration, an Undesirable Discharge is identical to a Bad Conduct Discharge. In addition there is an obvious effect on employment opportunities, as what we have said about General Discharges is applicable here.

If [the serviceman] is returned to civilian life with an Undesirable Discharge, his employability is jeopardized, not merely because gov-

---

[19] For an excellent discussion of punitive discharges, see Richard J. Bednar, "Discharge and Dismissal as Punishments in the Armed Services," *Military Law Review*, DA Pam 27–100–16 (April 1, 1962), pp. 1–42.

[20] Susskind, *op. cit.*, p. 25.

[21] Dougherty and Lynch, *op. cit.*, p. 517.

ernmental and military jobs are closed to him, but because most employers insist on seeing a job hunter's discharge papers. The person discharged under AFR 35–66 (homosexuality) not only must reveal that his discharge was under conditions other than honorable, but his Report of Separation (Defense Department Form 214) specifically states the reason and authority (regulation number) for separation. In other words, he is branded as a homosexual.[22]

In a less clinical vein, we have the following statement from the Catholic War Veterans; referring to ". . . the terrifying instrument that destroys job acceptability," they say:

Thousands upon thousands of America's young men are turned away every year by civilian, government, and State employment offices because industry and government consider these discharged men as undesirable. They must show their discharge certificate that condemns them.[23]

Not only are jobs affected; the results of having such a discharge are claimed to have wider ramifications for the person's social situation. According to Congressman Clyde Doyle, the stigma of an Undesirable Discharge is equivalent to that of a Dishonorable Discharge.

I think it is, because with the ordinary person you will say a man is an undesirable citizen in civilian life, that is a life stigma. He is an undesirable. You don't want to have anything to do with him. You don't go into detail to find out what makes him undesirable. You think he may be a thief, he may be a homosexual, he may not be supporting his children, his family in the minds of some people, but he is undesirable, you don't want him around. And I think the ordinary patriotic sound thinking American citizen doesn't want to have anything to do with an undesirable man and that applies to an undesirable man from the military; something has occurred there in the

---

22 West and Glass, *op. cit.*, pp. 260–61.
23 Letter from Mr. A. F. Zerbee, Counsel, Catholic War Veterans, United States of America, to 1966 Subcommittee Hearings, March 7, 1966, reproduced *ibid.*, pp. 834–35. Included also are excerpts from letters of people detailing the employment difficulties they have undergone on account of having Undesirable Discharges.

military for which he has got an undesirable discharge, it is a stigma. It is a liability and a heavy one.[24]

Two important points are raised in the preceding statement. First, an Undesirable Discharge is a "life stigma." This not only means that it affects all areas of a person's life but that it is a label that continually accompanies him with a potential that is ever disruptive. Dougherty and Lynch speak of the serviceman's Undesirable Discharge as always remaining "part of his basic credentials";[25] and the Catholic War Veterans state that "the stigma is designed to last throughout the life of the former serviceman and only the Discharge Review Board or the Secretary of that branch of the service can change it."[26]

Second, there are the implications involved in being defined as "undesirable." It is unlikely that employers or neighbors will attempt to ascertain in what way an ex-serviceman was adjudged "undesirable." They will rather fill in the gaps themselves, basing their judgment on either what secondary information they have at hand or on pure flights of imagination. As such, the issuance of an Undesirable Discharge has been called "a flagrant act of character assassination."[27] Undesirable Discharges can be given for many violations, including fraudulent enlistment, prolonged unauthorized absence, drug addiction, established patterns of shirking, and established patterns of failing to pay just debts.[28] Thus an unfortunate outcome of being labeled "undesirable" is often being attributed secondary characteristics that are far removed from the truth. One important attribution has been commented on thus:

. . . an undesirable discharge today . . . no matter what the person has been discharged for—it might have been because he is mentally deficient—just a nit-wit, carries with it the suspicion of homosexuality,

---

[24] Statement made at the 1962 Subcommittee Hearings, p. 188.
[25] Dougherty and Lynch, *op. cit.*, p. 518.
[26] See note 23 above.
[27] *Ibid.*
[28] See Department of Defense directive 1332.14 of January 14, 1959, reprinted in 1966 Hearings, pp. 769–73; also, for Undesirable Discharges, Susskind, *op. cit.*, p. 26.

almost invariably. This question arises when a person has an undesirable discharge.[29]

Enough has been said, we feel, to demonstrate the stigmatic potential of an Undesirable Discharge, the discharge that most homosexuals separated from the services receive.

---

[29] Statement made by Joseph M. Snee, S.J., Professor, Georgetown University Law School, Washington, D.C., at 1966 Subcommittee Hearings, p. 335.

Chapter 3

THE EXTENT OF THE "PROBLEM"

GETTING PERSPECTIVE: DISCHARGES AS A WHOLE

Most service personnel leave with Honorable Discharges; at least 90 percent complete their time without difficulty, whether this is due to their behavior or good luck. Those who leave with General or Undesirable Discharges are about 5 to 6 percent of all discharges, and those who receive Bad Conduct or Dishonorable Discharges are about 1 percent or less of all discharges. There are fluctuations in these figures, but they have remained fairly stable at least over the period from 1951 to 1965. Before looking at what statistics we have on homosexual discharges, it might be useful to look at trends and numbers of discharges for each service over the recent past in order to obtain perspective.

The figures reported and discussed are those supplied by the various services to the 1962 and 1966 Subcommittee Hearings. No indication was given as to how they were collected, and for many questions asked by the Subcommittee, statistics just did not exist. The tables that follow are not always similar to those that appeared in the Subcommittee's report. For discharges, in general, tables are sometimes rearranged in an effort to make them comparable with other tables. In regard to this, percentages were also calculated where possible to make for ease of comparison (much of the data provided by the services were raw frequencies). Tables that deal with discharges for homosexuality originally included, in some cases, other reasons for the type of discharge; for ease of presentation these other data are omitted. Most tables throughout this section combine the results that appear separately in the 1962 and 1966 Subcommittee reports.

ARMY

Table 1 shows all enlisted administrative separations from the Army, 1951–65; and Table 2, punitive separations for the same

Table 1. Department of the Army Enlisted Administrative Separations 1951–65

YEAR	ENLISTED STRENGTH END FISCAL YEAR	TOTAL DISCHARGED	HONORABLE†	%	GENERAL	%	UNDESIRABLE	%	RETIREMENTS (ALL TYPES)
1951	—	116,724	102,881	91.2	4,200	3.6	2,523	2.2	3,577
1952	1,446,266	441,924	412,582	94.9	13,087	2.9	5,194	1.2	6,565
1953	1,386,500	809,275	772,535	96.5	15,888	2.0	6,617	0.8	8,442
1954	1,274,803	605,600	556,441	93.0	26,674	3.9	12,179	2.0	6,822
1955	985,659	732,597	691,012	95.0	18,726	2.6	14,611	2.0	4,742
1956	905,711	426,719	394,594	93.3	10,785	2.5	11,877	2.8	3,709
1957	885,056	385,273	355,616	93.2	6,593	1.7	15,228	4.0	3,449
1958	792,508	414,715	381,906	93.2	7,814	1.9	17,514	4.2	4,467
1959	758,458	357,684	334,744	94.7	5,910	1.7	11,031	3.1	4,056
1960	770,112	247,921	224,835	92.3	10,178	4.1	7,474	3.0	4,590
1961*	756,932	283,464	254,046	92.4	11,889	4.2	8,319	2.9	8,007
1962	948,597	305,822	275,519	93.0	12,198	4.0	7,958	2.6	9,080
1963	865,768	378,263	341,418	94.4	11,658	3.1	8,490	2.2	15,473
1964	800,514	392,243	354,215	94.3	12,616	3.2	8,479	2.2	15,965
1965	854,929	307,244	269,562	93.3	13,925	4.5	8,561	2.8	13,838

SOURCE: 1962 Hearings, p. 852; 1963 Hearings, p. 1036. (Combined tables.)

* Years prior to 1961 do not include enlisted females in discharge data, since such data were not maintained. Strengths do include enlisted females.

† Includes discharged for immediate enlistment or reenlistment and discharged from enlisted status to accept commissions.

**Table 2. Department of the Army Punitive
Separations 1951–65**

YEAR	BAD CONDUCT	%	DISHONORABLE	%
1951	1,164	1.0	2,379	2.0
1952	1,744	0.4	2,452	0.6
1953	1,708	0.2	4,285	0.5
1954	1,644	0.3	4,840	0.8
1955	960	0.1	2,546	0.3
1956	2,214	0.5	3,742	0.9
1957	1,681	0.4	2,711	0.7
1958	1,321	0.3	1,692	0.4
1959	1,074	0.3	869	0.2
1960	802	0.3	648	0.3
1961*	693	0.3	510	0.2
1962	725	0.2	532	0.2
1963	764	0.2	463	0.1
1964	604	0.2	369	0.1
1965	787	0.3	271	0.1

SOURCE: 1962 Hearings, p. 853; 1966 Hearings, p. 1036.
(Combined tables.)
* Years prior to 1961 do not include enlisted females in
discharge data, since such data were not maintained.
Strengths do include enlisted females.

period. It is apparent that most discharges are Honorable. Of
other kinds of discharges, the percentage of punitive discharges
(Bad Conduct and Dishonorable) as compared with the total
number of all other types of discharges have remained rather
constant over the period, although a slight decline can be dis-
cerned. Trends for administrative discharges are not readily
apparent, but except for 1957 and 1958, when Undesirable Discharges peaked at 4.0 percent and 4.2 percent of total discharges
issued, this type of discharge has represented between 2 and 3
percent of total discharges. The drop after 1958 and consequent
stabilization was probably due to a change in the basis and
authority for the issuance of General and Undesirable Discharges
introduced by DOD directive No. 1332.14, January 14, 1959,
which "liberalized" issuance of discharges. After that date it was
possible to issue higher types of discharges for reasons (unsuitability, unfitness, etc.) that previously would have resulted in

less favorable type discharges. This probably also accounts for the increase in General Discharges from 1959 to a point where they appear to have stabilized between 3 and 4 percent of total discharges. Other important factors that might account for fluctuations over the years could be the reduction of personnel after the Korean War and various quality control programs introduced to maintain levels of competence in the face of personnel reduction.

NAVY

Like the Army, the Navy shows a decrease in the issuance of the least desirable type discharge (Table 3). In the past fifteen years the number of punitive discharges steadily declined from about 6000 (4.2 percent of total discharges) in 1950 to 950 (0.6 percent of total discharges) in 1965. Over the same period the percent of Undesirable Discharges has been fairly constant, at about 2.0 percent of total discharges and General Discharges at about 4.0 percent of total discharges.

MARINES

Table 4 shows trends in discharges for the Marine Corps. Here, punitive discharges went from a high of 2796 in 1955 (5.0 percent of all discharges and releases) to a modern low of 766 in 1965 (1.4 percent of all discharges and releases). Undesirable Discharges have also declined in absolute numbers in the recent past from 1901 in 1955 (3.4 percent of all discharges and releases) to 1003 in 1965 (1.9 percent of all discharges and releases). It might be expected that, as in the Army, General Discharges would show an increase. The data provided do not, however, separate General from Honorable Discharges.

AIR FORCE

The Air Force provided figures from 1957 on (Table 5). These show a general decline in all types of less than honorable discharge. For example, Dishonorable Discharges went from a high of 711 in 1957 (0.4 percent of all discharges and retirements) to a low of 33 in 1965 (0.01 percent of all discharges and retire-

Table 3. Enlisted Separations from Active Duty, U.S. Navy 1950–65

FISCAL YEAR	TOTAL U.S. NAVY STRENGTH	TOTAL SEPARATIONS	HONORABLE No.	%*	GENERAL No.	%	UNDESIRABLE No.	%	BAD CONDUCT No.	%	DISHONORABLE No.	%
1950	331,860	141,511	129,100	91.2	5,095	3.6	1,647	1.2	5,178	3.6	791	0.6
1951	661,639	91,579	82,367	89.9	4,912	5.4	1,398	1.5	2,532	2.8	370	0.4
1952	735,753	140,994	130,829	92.8	5,663	4.0	2,439	1.7	1,893	1.3	170	0.1
1953	706,375	157,675	148,355	94.0	3,270	2.0	2,863	1.8	3,112	1.9	75	0.0
1954	642,048	156,057	143,123	91.7	4,986	3.2	3,867	2.5	4,013	2.6	68	0.0
1955	579,864	232,093	214,035	92.0	12,126	5.2	3,529	1.5	3,127	1.3	76	0.0
1956	591,996	224,975	211,114	93.8	9,219	4.1	2,540	1.1	1,846	0.8	66	0.0
1957	597,859	153,912	142,329	92.5	5,431	3.5	3,882	2.5	2,220	1.4	50	0.0
1958	563,906	192,398	178,414	92.7	6,901	3.6	4,259	2.2	2,784	1.4	40	0.0
1959	552,221	155,310	142,117	91.5	7,346	4.7	3,846	2.5	1,971	1.3	30	0.0
1960	544,040	153,897	143,165	93.0	6,342	4.1	2,697	1.7	1,663	1.1	30	0.0
1961	551,603	154,359	143,990	93.3	5,866	3.8	2,972	1.9	1,521	0.9	10	0.0
1962	584,071	164,693	154,138	93.6	6,809	4.1	2,474	1.5	1,261	0.8	11	0.0
1963	583,596	167,230	158,398	94.7	5,141	3.0	2,535	1.5	1,154	0.7	2	0.0
1964	584,750	166,539	157,658	94.7	4,735	2.8	3,142	1.9	1,002	0.6	2	0.0
1965	587,183	165,276	156,045	94.4	5,425	3.2	2,854	1.7	947	0.6	5	0.0

SOURCE: 1966 Hearings, p. 1001.

* The Percentages given by the Navy referred to percentage of total strength. The data have been recomputed by the authors so that percentages refer to percentage of total separations.

Table 4. U.S. Marine Corps—Selected Discharges and Average Enlisted Strength, Fiscal Years 1950–65 Inclusive

FISCAL YEAR	TOTAL DISCHARGES AND RELEASES HONORABLE AND GENERAL		UNDESIRABLE DISCHARGES		PUNITIVE DISCHARGES		TOTAL NUMBER OF DISCHARGES AND RELEASES
	No.	%*	No.	%	No.	%	
1950	32,779	95.4	579	1.1	1,166	3.4	34,324
1951	26,592	95.6	514	1.8	700	2.5	27,806
1952	39,364	96.1	880	2.2	700	1.7	40,944
1953	38,133	93.7	1,262	3.1	1,268	3.1	40,663
1954	56,437	93.7	1,551	2.3	2,268	3.8	60,256
1955	51,672	91.7	1,901	3.4	2,796	5.0	56,369
1956	65,302	93.7	1,873	2.7	2,537	3.6	69,712
1957	72,215	95.7	1,462	1.9	1,787	2.4	75,464
1958	54,744	95.0	1,375	2.4	1,458	2.5	57,577
1959	62,845	95.8	1,486	2.3	1,227	1.9	65,588
1960	50,339	94.4	1,868	3.5	1,114	1.8	53,321
1961	29,074	92.1	1,604	5.0	881	2.8	31,559
1962	40,407	94.2	1,482	3.5	982	2.3	42,871
1963	50,169	95.9	1,310	2.5	821	1.6	52,300
1964	57,915	96.3	1,288	2.1	913	1.5	60,116
1965	51,821	96.7	1,003	1.9	766	1.4	53,590

SOURCE: 1962 Hearings, p. 891; 1966 Hearings, p. 1004. (Combined table.)
* Percentages are of total number of all discharges and releases for the year in question and were computed by the authors.

Table 5. Air Force—Character of Discharges or Service of Enlisted Personnel 1957–65

FISCAL YEAR	1957		1958		1959		1960		1961		1962		1963		1964		1965	
	N	%*	N	%	N	%	N	%	N	%	N	%	N	%	N	%	N	%
TOTAL ENLISTED STRENGTH	776,566		735,759		704,562		680,666		689,557		746,185		732,626		720,372		690,177	
TOTAL DISCHARGES	193,409		197,679		177,740		154,521		187,884		176,556		126,340		181,598		215,759	
Honorable	169,141	87.4	171,293	86.6	157,408	88.5	135,657	87.7	169,995	90.4	160,335	90.8	104,204	82.4	161,683	89.0	195,620	90.6
General	11,347	5.8	12,664	6.4	7,380	4.1	7,246	4.7	7,160	3.8	6,037	3.4	6,158	4.8	4,671	2.6	4,407	2.0
Undesirable	7,214	3.7	8,300	4.2	7,124	4.0	4,189	2.7	1,699	0.9	1,295	0.7	1,220	0.9	848	0.5	781	0.4
Bad Conduct	2,470	1.2	2,267	1.1	1,522	0.8	1,342	0.8	1,057	0.6	412	0.2	324	0.2	290	0.1	224	0.1
Dishonorable	711	0.4	428	0.2	244	0.1	207	0.1	119	0.0	120	0.0	63	0.0	66	0.0	33	0.0
Retirements	2,526	1.3	2,727	1.3	4,062	2.2	5,880	3.8	7,854	4.1	8,357	4.7	14,371	4.7	14,040	7.7	14,694	6.8

SOURCE: 1962 Hearings, pp. 927, 947; 1966 Hearings, pp. 1045–1046. (Combined table.)
* Percentages are of total number of all discharges and retirements for the year in question and were computed by the authors.

ments), and Undesirable Discharges from a high of 8300 in 1958 (4.2 percent of all retirements and discharges) to a low of 781 in 1965 (0.4 percent of all retirements and discharges). Similar reductions can also be seen in Bad Conduct and General Discharges. The Air Force gave the following reasons for these trends to the Subcommittee: (a) the increase in percentage of career personnel, (b) more selective enlistment criteria, (c) earlier identification of characteristics showing inability to adjust to service life, and (d) the more liberal criteria in determining type of discharge introduced by the directive of 1959.

STATISTICS RELATING TO DISCHARGE FOR HOMOSEXUALITY

It is obvious from reading the Subcommittee Hearings that all services were unable (or unwilling) to produce data on numerous points regarding discharge procedures.[1] The data they had were often incomplete and, unfortunately for our purposes, not very detailed. Thus there are no tables that can be reproduced which show for all the services the number of persons discharged for homosexuality per year, and what type of discharge they received. We shall, therefore, have to put together as best we can an estimate from the data available.

According to Menninger, few military personnel were discharged from the armed forces for homosexuality during World War II. In 1943, for example, of 20,620 persons diagnosed as constitutional psychopaths by the Army, 1625 were of the "homosexual type."[2] A later set of official statistics shows that 4380 cases involving charges of "sexual perversion" were handled by the

---

[1] On the basis of detailed inquiries to the Surgeons General of the three major services, a psychiatrist reports that "there are no recent, reliable statistics indicating the number of persons currently disqualified for military duty or separated from the Armed Forces because of homosexuality." William M. Sheppe, Jr., "The Problem of Homosexuality in the Armed Forces," *Medical Aspects of Human Sexuality*, 3 (October 1969), 72.

[2] William C. Menninger, *Psychiatry in a Troubled World: Yesterday's War and Today's Challenge* (New York: Macmillan, 1948), p. 225.

military from January 1, 1947, to October 31, 1950.[3] These data come from evidence given by the armed services to a Senate subcommittee investigating the employment of homosexuals in government. The data, in Table 6, show about 1000 discharges per year for "sexual perversion" over the period.

Table 6. Sex Perversion Cases in the Armed Services (Military Personnel)

	NUMBER OF SEX PERVERSION CASES HANDLED		
	Jan. 1, 1947, through Mar. 31, 1950	Apr. 1, 1950, through Oct. 31, 1950	Total
Army	1,104	301	1,405*
Navy	1,665	399	2,064
Air Force	476†	435	911
Total	3,245	1,135	4,380

SOURCE: U.S. Congress, Senate Committee on Expenditures in the Executive Departments, Subcommittee on Investigations, "Employment of Homosexuals and Other Sex Perverts in Government," 1950. Appendix II (adapted).
* Included a few separations resulting from rape charges.
† Air Force figures included with Army until separation of records of these two services in January 1948.

It can be seen from the statistics that the Navy is overrepresented in the number of discharges for this offense when total strengths of the services are taken into consideration. Finally, West and Glass report an unofficial estimate that nearly 10,000 homosexual cases were handled by the services from November 1, 1950, to December 31, 1955.[4] These data suggest that something like 2000 persons per year were being separated from the armed forces for homosexuality between the late forties and mid-fifties. This figure is also suggested by the Society for Individual Rights, a homophile society.

---

[3] U.S. Congress, Senate, Committee on Expenditure in the Executive Departments, Subcommittee on Investigations, "Employment of Homosexuals and Other Sex Perverts in Government" (1950).
[4] Louis Jolyon West and Albert J. Glass, "Sexual Behavior and the Military Law," in Ralph Slovenko (ed.), *Sexual Behavior and the Law* (Springfield, Ill.: Charles C Thomas, 1965), pp. 267–68.

No one knows how many of the approximately three million service-men on active duty have been investigated or discharged for homosexuality. Defense Department officials say no figures are available. But unofficial estimates dating back to the early 1950's suggest that an average of 2,000 persons (i.e., 1 out of every 1,500 servicemen or less than one tenth of one percent of all service personnel) are so discharged each year.[5]

Whose "unofficial" estimates these are is not mentioned. However, keeping this estimate in mind, let us look at the figures provided by the services to the Subcommittee Hearings. Among the questions asked by the Subcommittee was a partial break-down of "the basis, reason or authority" for the issuance of discharges. It was obvious from replies that such statistics were not kept by all services or, if they were, were often put under legal categories that obscured specific cause. The following statistics were presented.

ARMY

Table 7 shows what appear to be the number of Class III homosexuals separated from the Army in 1964–65. These 606 persons, it also appears, had not requested a board hearing but had waived the right and accepted whatever discharge they were given. No indication is given in this table or elsewhere as to the number of Class II homosexuals who were administratively discharged with Undesirable Discharges. Neither is any information supplied on Class I homosexuals over the period. The only information on Army enlisted personnel separated for homosexual offenses, therefore, covers two years, and pertains only to Class III homosexuals. Of these it is impossible to say how many received Honorable and how many General Discharges.

The Army did not record the number of enlisted personnel separated because of homosexuality until mid-1960. Recent data, supplied by Sheppe, report that for the seven and one-half year period (1960–67), 6139 enlisted men were separated for homo-

---

[5] Society for Individual Rights, *The Armed Forces and Homosexuality* (San Francisco: Society for Individual Rights, no date), unpaged.

**Table 7. Enlisted Personnel: Administrative Discharges
1964–65 (Army)**

	FISCAL YEAR 1964		FISCAL YEAR 1965	
	Under Honorable Conditions*	Undesirable	Under Honorable Conditions*	Undesirable
Unsuitability Reason:				
Acceptance of discharge (Class III homosexual)	166	†	211	†
Homosexual tendencies	119	†	110	†

SOURCE: 1966 Hearings, p. 919.
* Includes both Honorable and General Discharges.
† Not authorized.

sexuality, an average of 818 per year.[6] Presumably, these would
be mainly Class II homosexuals.

Table 8 refers to officers and covers the period 1957–65. It

**Table 8. Officers: Resignations in Lieu of Board Action
1957–65 (Army)**

	OTHER THAN HOMOSEXUAL		HOMOSEXUAL	
	Regular Army	Reserve	Regular Army	Reserve
1957	6	119	8	50
1958	2	51	6	23
1959	5	44	8	22
1960	—	17	4	10
1961	1	18	6	21
1962	(data lost)	(data lost)	(data lost)	(data lost)
1963	8	33	5	17
1964	7	36	4	30
1965	5	32	8	14

SOURCE: 1962 Hearings, p. 853; 1966 Hearings, p. 1036. (Combined table.)

deals only with resignations in lieu of board action, however, and
not separations under any other procedure. It can be readily seen
that under 10 cases per year are so separated from the regular

[6] Sheppe, *op. cit.,* p. 72.

Army, whereas with regard to the reserves the numbers fluctuate from a high of 50 in 1957 to a low of 10 in 1960, with an average of a little over 20 per year for the period. Between 1957 and 1965 the average annual number of officer separations (excluding 1962) for homosexuality from the Army is 30.

NAVY

For the Navy the situation is somewhat clearer. Although we have no data on those separated with General Discharges or punitive discharges for homosexuality, we do have the numbers of enlisted men given Undesirable Discharges for homosexuality for 1950–65 (Table 9). This shows that 17,392 enlisted men were

Table 9. U.S. Navy Undesirable Discharges
(Enlisted Personnel)

FISCAL YEAR	HOMOSEXUAL	ALL UNDESIRABLE
1950	483	1,647
1951	533	1,398
1952	1,352	2,439
1953	1,335	2,863
1954	1,020	3,867
1955	833	3,529
1956	933	2,540
1957	1,307	3,882
1958	1,244	4,259
1959	1,223	3,846
1960	958	2,697
1961	1,148	2,972
1962	1,175	2,474
1963	1,162	2,535
1964	1,321	3,142
1965	1,365	2,854

SOURCE: 1962 Hearings, p. 913; 1966 Hearings, pp. 1001, 1002. (Combined table.)

so discharged over the 16-year period, an annual average of 1087. No such statistics are available for officers.

MARINES

Table 10 shows Undesirable Discharges given by the Marine Corps on the grounds of unfitness and misconduct for homo-

**Table 10. Marine Corps Undesirable Discharges
(Enlisted Personnel, 1960–65)**

Unfitness	1960	1961	1962	1963	1964	1965
Lewd acts	23	41	34	30	9	8
Homosexual acts	129	159	72	40	27	29
Sodomy	52	108	274	292	226	208
Misconduct						
Preservice homosexual acts	55	25	46	42	53	55
Total Undesirable	1,868	1,604	1,482	1,310	1,288	1,003

SOURCE: 1962 Hearings, p. 913; 1966 Hearings, p. 1004. (Combined table.)

sexual related acts 1960–65. For preservice homosexual acts, presumably Class III homosexuals, the figure is about 40 to 50 per year (the annual average is 46 for the period). For homosexual acts the figure goes from a high of 159 in 1961 to a low of 27 in 1964, an annual average of 76. Two other categories have also been included—lewd acts and sodomy—which could include homosexual offenses, but how many is unknown. The Marine Corps does state, however, that a substantial majority of its Undesirable Discharges are given for homosexual acts and for convictions by civil authorities.[7]

In 1961, for example, the Marine Corps stated that homosexuality and other sexual perversions account for approximately 18 percent of all its Undesirable Discharges, whereas the figure was 40 percent for the Navy.[8] (Given this figure, approximately 289 persons received Undesirable Discharges from the Marines for these offenses in 1961; for the Navy the comparable figure would be 1188, which is close to the calculated annual average of 1087.) If this trend was stable, then we would expect that some 200 to 300 persons have received Undesirable Discharges for homosexuality per year since the early 1950s. This does not include officers; here again no statistics are available.

---

[7] 1966 Subcommittee Hearings, p. 1006.
[8] 1962 Subcommittee Hearings, p. 894.

AIR FORCE

Here again statistics are woefully inadequate for our purposes. Table 11 appeared in 1962 and purported to represent types of

Table 11. Air Force Separations for Homosexuality 1965

1965	HONORABLE	GENERAL	UNDESIRABLE	TOTAL
Homosexuality	109	332	350	791

SOURCE: 1966 Hearings, p. 1046.

discharges given for homosexual related offenses for 1960. The same table appeared in 1966, this time being said to refer to the year 1965. For what it is worth, it shows that most such offenders received Undesirable Discharges. The table most likely refers to 1960, however, and there has been a misprint as it does not jibe with other data available. A better table is Table 12, which shows

Table 12. Administrative Discharges—Air Force 1962–65
Class II Homosexuals

	1962	1963	1964	1965	TOTAL
General	221	258	225	247	951
Undesirable	268	299	235	245	1,047
Total	489	557	460	492	1,998

SOURCE: 1966 Hearings, p. 967 (table reorganized by authors).

the number of Class II homosexuals for 1962 through 1965 and the type of discharge they received. As far as less than honorable discharges are concerned, about 500 per year on average were issued over this period. Again we have no data on other classes of homosexual or on officer separations.

The data provided by the military are so incomplete that it seems worthless to attempt an annual estimate. Changes in policy make for large jumps in the figures, and in some cases we have data for only a limited period.[9] However, an estimate was made

---

[9] The problems involved in extrapolation from limited time periods are seen in current Navy statistics. Sheppe remarks that there has been a re-

which, if many assumptions are held, does not depart too far from the 2000 per year suggested. This is shown in Table 13. As

Table 13. Estimated Average Number of Less Than Honorable Discharges for Homosexuality Per Year for Each Service

SERVICE	CLASS I	CLASS II	CLASS III	OFFICERS	TOTAL
Army	—	568[a]	250[b]	30[c]	848
Navy	—	1,087[d]	—	—	1,087
Marines	—	200[e]	46[f]	—	246
Air Force	—	499[g]	—	—	499
					2,680

[a] Based on Sheppe's figures for 1960–67 minus [b] on the assumption that not all these persons were Class II homosexuals.

[b] Table 7. Six hundred and six persons separated for homosexuality, 1964–65, gives an average of about 300 per year. Not all received less than honorable discharges, however; the estimate is based on the assumption that the majority received General Discharges.

[c] Table 8. This includes only those officers resigning in lieu of board action. This number is obtained from averaging over the period 1957–65.

[d] Table 9. This figure includes only those who received Undesirable Discharges, 1950–65. We are assuming here that the majority of these persons were Class II homosexuals.

[e] Table 10. Gives an annual average of 76 for Marine personnel given Undesirable Discharges for homosexual acts 1960–65, presumably Class II homosexuals. The Marine Corps also stated, however, that homosexuality and other sexual perversions accounted for 18 percent of all its Undesirable Discharges in 1961, giving a total of 289 persons so discharged for that date. It is difficult to choose an estimate between these two figures. However, it is assumed that an annual average of 200 is a correct approximation.

[f] Table 10. Gives us an annual average of 46 for Marine personnel given Undesirable Discharges for Preservice Homosexual Acts 1960–65. These cases are assumed to be mainly Class III homosexuals.

[g] Table 12. Gives an annual average of 499 Class II homosexuals separated from the Air Force between 1962 and 1965.

can be seen, we get a total annual average of 2680 from these figures without including any Class I persons and including officers from only one service branch. These cases, plus those

markable decline in separations for homosexuality beginning in 1966. This is apparently due to the increasing concern given to drug problems by naval authorities, which have resulted in less attention to homosexual offenses. Sheppe, *op. cit.*, p. 73.

Class III cases that we could not estimate, do not constitute large numbers.

To conclude, we would suggest that in recent times an average annual estimate of those persons separated from the armed forces with less than honorable discharges for homosexuality-connected reasons would be not fewer than 2000 per year, with the upper limit probably not exceeding 3000.

Chapter 4

THE HOMOSEXUAL IN THE MILITARY
ENVIRONMENT

THE MILITARY COMMUNITY

The chief characteristic of military life is its bureaucratic structure, typified by a sharply defined hierarchy of authority and privilege and by a highly refined, internal specialization of tasks.[1]

The bureaucratic structure of the military functions to provide for all the basic physical needs of its members so that life can be lived within the confines of the organization. As such, military institutions provide the archetype for what Goffman calls "total institutions": "a place of residence and work where a large number of like-situated individuals, cut off from the wider society for an appreciable period of time, together lead an enclosed, formally administered round of life."[2]

In order to achieve their goals, total institutions engage in a variety of behaviors to strip away the old identities of their members and provide them instead with identities consonant with the efficient running of the organization.[3] Thus, for the military, this involves replacing the civilian identity of the new recruit with the identity of soldier.[4]

---

[1] Arthur J. Vidich and Maurice R. Stein, "The Dissolved Identity in Military Life," in Maurice R. Stein, Arthur J. Vidich, and David Manning White (eds.), *Identity and Anxiety: Survival of the Person in Mass Society* (New York: Free Press, 1960), p. 493.

[2] Erving Goffman, *Asylums: Essays on the Social Situation of Mental Patients and Other Inmates* (Garden City, N.Y.: Doubleday, Anchor Books, 1961), Introduction.

[3] This process, which Goffman calls "mortification of the self," is described by him in "On the Characteristics of Total Institutions," *op. cit.*, pp. 3–124.

[4] How this is done is described by Vidich and Stein, *op. cit.*, pp. 497–505.

It is possible to view the internal dynamics of total institutions whose membership is involuntary as the product of the struggle between those in authority who wish to impose a new identity or role and those novitiates who wish to retain aspects of their previous identities and roles. Thus we often find on the part of the lower participants[5] certain nonofficial "secondary adjustments" to pressures from above.[6] These adjustments can be personal—for example, minor sabotage and "goldbricking"—or can be group supported—for example, common nicknames for higher personnel and covering up mistakes made by group members. How frequent and serious the effects of these deviant adjustments are will be partly a function of the surveillance system of the organization. It is a characteristic of total institutions that surveillance is extensive; in addition, because of the bureaucratically organized specialization of tasks and hierarchy of authority, it becomes easy not only to state who is responsible for what but also who is responsible to whom. Thus infractions that concern noncompletion of tasks and disobedience to orders stand out in relief against the ordered day-to-day operations of the organization.

Surveillance is especially extensive in military institutions, where discipline is highly valued. Thus, on the base, the opportunities for deviance are often limited—there are a multiplicity of rules that govern a variety of contingencies which the soldier is required to know; his time is accounted for down to the last minute; his personal effects are subject to daily inspection; he lacks privacy; and he sees that infractions are difficult to hide and that punishment swiftly follows. His major opportunity for deviant behavior lies in those occasions when he can leave the

---

5 This term which describes those low in power and prestige within organizations comes from Etzioni. See Amitai Etzioni, *A Comparative Analysis of Complex Organizations* (New York: Free Press, 1961).

6 Goffman, *op. cit.*, p. 189: "Secondary adjustments" are "any habitual arrangement by which a member of an organization employs unauthorized means, or obtains unauthorized ends, or both, thus getting around the organization's assumptions as to what he should do and get and hence what he should be."

base, but here the surveillance of civilian authorities supports the
efforts of the military to control its members in civilian settings.

SEX AND THE MILITARY

No matter how much reworking of a serviceman's social psychological makeup the military can do, it cannot alter to any
great degree his basic drives. Thus, insofar as sexual drives and
energies are concerned, these are little altered in the transition
from civilian to soldier. This presents no problem to the military,
unless these drives affect efficiency, discipline, or morale. The
military's concern has been mainly with homosexuality and vene-
real disease, which it defines as problematic in the above respects.

There are two important facts about the military situation
where sex is concerned. First, there is an all-male environment, so
that members, the majority of whom are heterosexual, can find no
sexual outlet within the organization. Second, no sexual outlets
are provided at all by the military organization. Unlike other
armies, the U.S. Army discourages camp followers, and only in
times of war, outside the United States itself, does it tolerate
specific military brothels.

In such situations, therefore, sexual drives can be handled
either by suppression (abstinence), autoeroticism, homosexuality, heterosexual sex of some kind, or numerous psychological
substitutes. Both Kinsey and Ehrmann provide data that show
patterns of heterosexual behavior to be little altered among men
in the armed forces during times of war.[7] For example, for those
who had their first heterosexual experience in the armed forces,
the probability is that most would have done likewise at that age
if they had not been in service; the men who had most heterosexual sex in the armed forces were those who probably would
have had most heterosexual sex if they had stayed at home.

Granted, though, the situation is exacerbated in the all-male

---

[7] Alfred C. Kinsey, Wardell B. Pomeroy, and Clyde E. Martin, *Sexual Behavior in the Human Male* (Philadelphia: Saunders, 1948), p. 416.
Winston Ehrmann, *Pre-marital Dating Behavior* (New York: Holt,
1959).

setting because of the great value placed on "masculinity" by authorities and the men themselves. This leads to certain symbolic manifestations of virility and toughness in the military setting such as excessive drinking, profanity, and a concern with sex expressed in such things as pinups, jokes, and bragging.[8] Even if behavior does not radically change, it can be suggested that the erotic situation does, in that sex is made much more relevant and pervasive in the all-male military setting than it would be for the person outside it.

It is this that seems to bother military authorities. Cut off from fiancée, girl friend, or wife, and subject to an environment that gives great importance to sex, will the soldier attempt release through expedient homosexual behavior? This is a problem that worries not only military authorities.

The lack of opportunity to establish contacts with females . . . denies the men a normal outlet for erotic impulses and affectionate feelings. This introduces a source of conflict in the development of intense feelings of friendship toward fellow recruits; specifically the fear that one's affectionate tendencies, now directed exclusively toward males with whom one lives in intimate, daily contact, might be contaminated by erotic feelings.[9]

One way this conflict is resolved, according to Janis, is by participation in "homosexual buffoonery" in which the homosexual role is aped in a spirit of play; thus, the behavior which it symbolizes is neutralized by considering it in nonserious terms.

Elkin reports a similar observation, but interprets it differently:

Although there was continual joking about homosexual practices, there was an apparent total lack of awareness of homosexual attitudes and inclinations such as were extremely widespread in a latent, and not uncommon in a practiced, but verbally unadmitted, state.[10]

For Janis, the participants were aware of their feelings; for Elkin,

---

[8] See Henry Elkin, "Aggressive and Erotic Tendencies in Army Life," *American Journal of Sociology,* 51 (March 1946), 408–13.

[9] Irving L. Janis, "Psychodynamic Aspects of Adjustment to Army Life," *Psychiatry,* 8 (May 1945), 170.

[10] Elkin, *op. cit.,* p. 412.

apparently, they were not. Whether aware or not, the important point is whether homosexual sex occurred. According to Bieber, it does not; referring to the major psychiatric papers published during the war years, he says "none referred to expedient homosexual behavior despite the deprivation of women for millions of men."[11]

Of course there is a lot that psychiatrists could have missed, but the statement does seem consistent with what Kinsey and Ehrmann say about the effect of military life on sexual behavior. Kinsey's statement on the problem is worth quoting:

> There is a ready assumption that men in segregated groups, as in the Army and Navy, turn to the homosexual more often than they would at home; but it is to be recalled that the active incidence of the homosexual in the peacetime U.S. population among men of Army and Navy age is nearly 30%, and one would have to show that the incidence among men in the Army and Navy is higher than that, or that the frequencies of contact are higher, in order to prove that patterns for these men had been changed in any way. There are, of course, men who have their first homosexual experience while in the Army or Navy, but there are men of the same age who would have had their first experience at home if there had never been a war.[12]

It should be realized that we have been discussing research done during a period of war. Things might be different in times of peace. However, there seems to be little evidence to suggest that the extent of expedient homosexuality is at all widespread; if the heterosexual soldier does find sexual outlet a problem, homosexuality is not the major solution he chooses.

Some heterosexuals, however, do engage in homosexual behavior in the military, for which they are brought before authorities. For example, "rolling queers" for money, shower room horseplay, and, in some cases, for the prestige of being "blown" by a homosexual, an activity which among certain circles does not brand the receiver as homosexual as long as he takes no active part in it

---

[11] Irving Bieber et al., *Homosexuality: A Psychoanalytic Study* (New York: Basic Books, 1961), p. 308.
[12] Kinsey et al., *op. cit.*, p. 416.

and shows no affection for the fellator.[13] Another class of heterosexuals who engage in homosexual behavior are those who do so while under the influence of alcohol.[14] All these instances involve men for whom the activity is not expedient. Druss has described the typical heterosexual who is liable to be implicated in these behaviors.[15] He found them to be younger and less well educated than the true or confirmed homosexual and diagnosed them as having "immaturity reactions." He concludes: "For the most part these individuals were similar to the many soldiers referred for evaluation before separation from the military for unfitness or unsuitability."[16] He does not provide an answer as to why their immaturity should be manifested in homosexual acts. It is this type of person, no doubt, that the military has in mind when it talks about the homosexual seducing or corrupting other military personnel.

We have discussed the problem of homosexuality in the military so far with reference to four types: those for whom homosexuality is a latent phenomenon, those for whom homosexuality is expedient behavior, those for whom homosexuality is "accidental" behavior, and those for whom homosexuality is a result of immaturity. The persons we are most interested in, however, are those for whom homosexual behavior is a major form of sexual expression.

It is apparent that such homosexuality is far more frequent than once believed. Of the approximately 3 million servicemen on active duty in any one year, there must be a considerable number of homosexuals. At the least, this number must be greater than the 2000 to 3000 discharges per year for homosexuality which we

---

13 These phenomena among delinquent boys have been outlined in detail by Albert J. Reiss. See Albert J. Reiss, Jr., "The Social Integration of Queers and Peers," *Social Problems*, 9 (Fall 1961), 102–20.

14 For a description of some of these cases see Louis J. West, W. T. Doidge, and R. L. Williams, "An Approach to the Problem of Homosexuality in the Military Service," *American Journal of Psychiatry*, 115 (November 1958), 392–401.

15 Richard G. Druss, "Cases of Suspected Homosexuality Seen at an Army Mental Hygiene Consultation Service," *Psychiatric Quarterly*, 41 (January 1967), 62–70.

16 *Ibid.*, p. 66.

have estimated. We know, too, that over 90 percent of servicemen receive Honorable Discharges. It appears obvious, therefore,
that most homosexuals remain undiscovered by military authorities and complete their service with honor. Some evidence for
this point comes from Fry and Rostow.[17] Of 183 men known to
be homosexual prior to military service, they found that 51 were
rejected at induction. Of the remainder, only 14 were discharged
from the service—that is, 118 served from 1 to 5 years, of whom
58 percent became officers. This group was able to handle their
homosexuality throughout the period and make excellent records
for themselves. More recent research conducted by the Institute
for Sex Research in 1967 showed that of some 458 male homosexuals, 214 had served in the military, of whom 77 percent
received Honorable Discharges. Earlier data reported by Simon
and Gagnon indicate that only 20 percent of 550 white homosexual males who had served in the military reported any difficulties.[18] Finally, in the present study, of 136 homosexuals who
had served in the military, 76 percent received Honorable Discharges.[19]

---

[17] C. C. Fry and E. G. Rostow, *National Research Council*, interim report
OEM cmr, 337 (April 1, 1945), reported by William C. Menninger,
*Psychiatry in a Troubled World: Yesterday's War and Today's Chal-
lenge* (New York: Macmillan, 1948), p. 227. Another study which re-
ports on the good records and ability of homosexuals in the military is
Lewis J. Loesser, "The Sexual Psychopath in the Military Service: A
Study of 270 Cases," *American Journal of Psychiatry*, 102 (July 1945),
92–101.

[18] William Simon and John H. Gagnon, "Homosexuality: The Formulation
of a Sociological Perspective," *Journal of Health and Social Behavior*, 8
(September 1967), 180.

[19] One other fact that should be noted is, of course, that a proportion of
homosexuals do not serve at all either because they avoid induction or
are rejected at induction. How large this proportion is we do not know
for sure. Kinsey et al. report some figures from the Second World War
which state that less than 1 percent were turned down at induction
centers or rejected by draft boards for being "homosexual." They consider this to be too small an estimate, however, explained by the fact
that being turned down because of homosexuality was none too easy
to keep confidential; therefore, "few men with any common sense
would admit their homosexual experience to draft boards or to psychiatrists at induction centers or in the services." Kinsey, *op. cit.*, pp.
621–22.
   The only other estimate we could find as to the proportion of those

These findings should not be considered remarkable; to define them as such suggests a stereotyped view of the homosexual as having uncontrollable sex drives that demand constant satisfaction (a view implicitly held by military authorities). Most homosexuals, not unlike most heterosexuals, pursue sex according to rules that reduce visibility and potential risk. The homosexual realizes the consequences of homosexual behavior in the military; as the consequences have similarities to discovery in civilian settings, he is likely to apply the same type of operative rules that he had learned before.

What does the homosexual do? In some cases—although these we think are few—he abstains from sexual expression—especially where getting an Honorable Discharge is an important concern for him. In the majority of cases, we believe, his behavior is not radically altered from what it was in civilian life—if it is, it is toward reducing homosexual sex because of lack of privacy or lack of free time. For the homosexual who is based near a large city and who has free time, he may behave much the same, and as discreetly, as he did outside the military.

It is understandable that not more homosexuals are discovered in the military. If we put aside the common stereotypes of the homosexual and realize that he too—and probably more so than heterosexuals—is subject to the societal regulation of sexuality, then by keeping to his own places and with a certain amount of discretion, he can substantially reduce the risk of discovery. What these risks are and what contingencies surround discovery are considered later.

---

persons who avoid the draft comes from a reported statement by Col. Robert A. Bier, chief medical officer for the national Selective Service System, who, in a study of 1,500,000 men called for examination between 1960 and 1962, found that 382,000 (25.4 percent) were granted medical deferments. Psychiatric disorders including homosexuality accounted for 11 percent of the latter. What proportion homosexuality was of psychiatric disorders was not mentioned. (*Time* magazine, March 15, 1968, p. 15.) Estimates after this date should be read with caution, as homosexuality has been used as an excuse to avoid the draft on the part of some of those opposed to the Vietnam War. See "How Faked Faggotry Can Lead to Your Honorable Discharge," *The Realist*, 76 (January 1968), 11–12, 14.

Chapter 5

METHODOLOGY

RESEARCH DESIGN

The two main questions which this research addresses are (1) What are the sociosexual factors related to the process of discovery (which eventuates in a less than honorable discharge for reasons of homosexuality)? and (2) What are the social and psychological effects of receiving a less than honorable discharge?

To answer these questions adequately it is necessary to utilize some form of experimental design. Ideally this would involve:[1]

(a) Two groups, experimental and control, equalized at time 1 (prior to induction) by matching or some randomization procedure so that the effects of extraneous variables are minimized.

(b) Control over the test factor (in the instance of question 2 this would be type of discharge) that would be "applied" only to the experimental group which would be compared at a later date, time 2, with the control group.

It is obvious that such conditions cannot be obtained in the present research. First, we are unable to randomly constitute two groups as our experimental and control groups and, second, we have no control over the test factors. We can only come upon the scene at time 2, therefore, and retrospectively reconstruct the events of interest. In other words, we have to adopt a less rigorous design than classical experimental design, an ex post facto design of some sort.

---

[1] For a discussion of experimental designs in sociology and their limitations, see Matilda White Riley, *Sociological Research* (New York: Harcourt, Brace & World, 1963); and Travis Hirschi and Hannan C. Selvin, *Delinquency Research: An Appraisal of Analytic Methods* (New York: Free Press, 1967).

The major limitation of such designs is asserting with confidence that the groups being compared were equal in important respects at time 1. In addition to those variables that might have caused inequality between the groups at time 1 and whose effects cannot be randomized, other uncontrolled variables could be at work during the period between times 1 and 2, so that effects attributed to the independent variable could be the effects of another, unknown variable. The issue is one of adequate control in order to make "cause and effect" assertions. (With our research, for example, findings attributed to the effects of discharge could in fact be predisposing elements in getting caught in the first place—for example, "swishy" behavior and other aspects cited as secondary deviance.)

SAMPLE

Our sample was selected with the following intention: first, to obtain a large number of male homosexuals; second, to ignore those who had not had military experience; and finally, from those that had, to select, first, those who had received less than honorable discharges and, second, to choose from the remainder a group to act as controls.

This strategy was carried out in the following way. The cooperation of the Mattachine Society of New York was obtained—especially permission to use the names and addresses on their mailing and membership lists. From these lists, those persons who lived in the New York metropolitan area were selected out. The final number of persons established for the New York area was 872. At the end of March 1968 a one-page questionnaire was sent to each of these people.

This questionnaire (Questionnaire 1—see Appendix 1) was designed to do two things: (1) to collect basic information from each subject; (2) to get permission for an interview. Each person who would agree to an interview was asked to put his name, address, and telephone number on the questionnaire and a time when he could be most easily reached.

From these data we were able to create experimental and control groups and say something about their equivalence at time 1. Having established these two groups the intention was then to interview them (Interview Schedule—Appendixes 2 and 3) and, in addition, have them complete another questionnaire (Questionnaire 2—Appendix 4).

The returns from the New York sample were generally disappointing; they were as follows:

Sample Source: Mattachine Society of New York

Total number of questionnaires mailed	872
Total returned completed	220 (25.6%)
Total returned with either no permission for interview (i.e., unsigned) or no military experience (or both)	169
Total returned with both permission for interview and military experience	51

The 51 "useful" returns (5.8 percent of the number sent out) included 15 persons who had received a less than honorable discharge for homosexuality and 36 who had received Honorable Discharges from the forces. Three things became obvious from this return. First, to do a study at all it was essential that the majority of the 15 persons in the experimental group keep their promise to be interviewed. Second, that there were an insufficient number of control subjects to match them with the experimental subjects. Thus, the control group was chosen by randomly selecting 15 subjects out of the control "pool" of 36, giving us two groups of 15 subjects each. Finally, it was felt that efforts should be made to get subjects from other sample sources in order to increase the size of the sample.

With regard to the last point, we turned to the Society for Individual Rights (S.I.R.) in San Francisco, the largest homophile organization on the West Coast. We employed the same type of procedure in San Francisco as we had in New York. Questionnaires were sent to all members in the San Francisco area; these were mailed during the last week of July 1968. The returned questionnaires were picked up in San Francisco after the New York data had been collected. New York mailing was completed during March, and the majority of replies were received by early May. Interviewing was completed by early August, with every case honoring the commitment to be interviewed except one—unfortunately, an experimental group subject.

San Francisco replies were picked up in mid-August, and with the help of a research assistant, experimental and control groups were selected and interviewing was completed within three weeks. Five hundred questionnaires were sent out to S.I.R. members; the replies were as follows:

Sample Source: Society for Individual Rights, San Francisco

Total number of questionnaires mailed	500
Total returned completed	208 (41.6%)
Total returned with either no permission for interview (unsigned) or no military experience (or both)	123
Total returned with both permission for interview and military experience	85

The 85 "useful" returns (17 percent of the number sent out) included 17 persons who had received a less than honorable discharge from the military for reasons of homosexuality. Of the 68 remaining, 2 were excluded for having less than honorable discharges for reasons other than homosexuality, and from the remaining 66, 17 were randomly selected to form a control group.

The question might be raised as to why the response from the Society for Individual Rights (S.I.R.) was much better than that from Mattachine (M.S.N.Y.): 41.6 percent as against 25.6 percent. The following reasons are suggested:

1. The main reason was that S.I.R.'s membership list is better organized and more up to date. By better organized is meant that everyone on it is a bona fide member, and professional and non-homosexual members are clearly separated; furthermore, efforts are made to keep it up to date. Mattachine's list was not as well organized. First, although members are distinguished from people who are just on the mailing list, it was difficult (almost impossible) to find out who were professional members or non-homosexuals. The mailing list itself contained all sorts of people;

for example, it seemed an unofficial policy to put everyone who wrote or called for information on this list, so that not only did they get initial information about Mattachine but also later communications from the organization. Thus, as we found to our chagrin, this list included people who ranged from the student who had once done a term paper on homosexuality to those who wrote inflammatory letters to the organization calling them "filthy perverts" or promising them "the wrath of God." In addition, attempts had only just begun to keep their lists up to date; thus many persons had moved or died but were still on the list.

2. Next, members of S.I.R. were forewarned that they would be receiving a questionnaire in their official newsletter, "Gold-sheet." They were told who it was from, generally what it asked, that the board of directors had approved the mailing, and that they should cooperate in the research. At the time the research was done in New York it was not possible to put such a notice in the Mattachine Newsletter.

These two factors, we believe, were instrumental in getting not only a higher response rate from S.I.R. but also a larger number of respondents who were willing to put their names and addresses on the questionnaire—about 70 percent (145 out of 208) as compared with approximately 56 percent (123 out of 220) from M.S.N.Y. This latter fact could be due to each organization attracting a different type of homosexual (for example, the more secure and committed against those less so).[2]

Thus, in combination, our final sample consisted of 64 subjects, 32 each in the experimental and control groups. Unfortunately, as

---

[2] For a discussion of different sample sources of homosexuals and the characteristics of their respondents, see Martin S. Weinberg, "Homosexual Samples: Differences and Similarities," *Journal of Sex Research*, November 1970. Weinberg's data show a general lack of differences between sample sources in psychological adjustment (his sample sources included M.S.N.Y. and Mattachine of San Francisco, along with S.I.R.).

A further point of interest is that of the 428 questionnaires that were returned completed, 292 (68.2 percent) were unable to be used either due to the fact that the person had not served in the military or that he did not give permission to be interviewed. The former reason was the more prevalent—of the 428 replies, 268 (62.6 percent) gave names and addresses.

we mentioned before, one member of the New York experimental group, despite repeated call-backs, reneged on his willingness to be interviewed, thus giving us a total N of 63. In some tables also (those dealing with interview data mainly), our experimental group is reduced by one more to 30. This is because of another New York subject who, despite filling out both questionnaires, talking informally, and supplying us with official transcripts of his trial and separation from the service, refused to submit to the formal interview. Enough data were gathered about him, however, to merit his inclusion in the sample.

It is clear that we can make no claims of representativeness for our sample. What we have is an analytic sample, selected so as to examine the relationship between one major variable and its correlates; generalizations from our findings, therefore, are only suggestive.

One problem with our sample source is apparent. That is, in using members of homophile organizations we are stacking the cards against finding any differences between our groups at the present time. That is, there are difficulties in saying what the effects of a less than honorable discharge are when we are using as a control group honorable dischargees who identify enough as homosexuals to be involved in a homophile organization. In addition, some persons who received less than honorable discharges may have ceased their homosexual behavior. Both groups, therefore, are already involved in the homosexual world, which makes the effects of labeling more difficult to test.

REPLICATION

With regard to this problem, we were fortunate to have access to data from a more general study of 458 Chicago homosexuals carried out by the Institute for Sex Research in 1967. The study did not rely on homophile members for its sample, but selected male homosexuals from a variety of locales, with the result that only 20 percent of the respondents were members of a homophile organization. The Chicago sample represents a different segment of the homosexual population than our sample, so that any replication of our findings would add considerably to their strength.

Among the questions asked in the Chicago study was whether the respondent had been in military service, whether he had received an Honorable Discharge, and if not, did this have anything to do with homosexuality. In the sample it was found that 32 subjects received less than honorable discharges for homosexuality, and 164, Honorable Discharges. Since the latter group differed significantly from the former in age and education, respondents were randomly removed from various age and educational categories to provide a comparable group; the N in the Honorable Discharge group was reduced to 48.

CONSTRUCTION AND ADMINISTRATION OF THE QUESTIONNAIRES AND INTERVIEW

The instruments used in this study and the form they took were related to the theoretical questions previously raised. The two main instruments chosen for this task were two fixed-choice questionnaires and an open-ended interview.

QUESTIONNAIRE 1

As previously described, this was the questionnaire that was used to select the sample. It included the following sets of questions (their specific form can be seen in Appendix 1):

1. *Background information.* Age, occupation, income, education, religion, father's occupation, family income, race, marital status.

2. *Homosexual career.* Age when respondent experienced first homosexual orgasm; age respondent began regularly seeking homosexual partners; age respondent defined himself as homosexual.

3. *Service experience.* If the respondent had served; in what branch; for how long; the type of discharge received and if it was connected with homosexuality.

4. *Time 1 information.* If the respondent had served, then at the time of his induction (a) the proportion of his friends who were homosexual, (b) the extent of his homosexual activities, (c) how often he associated with homosexuals, (d) his perception of

his sexual orientation, (e) concern about exposure of his homo-sexuality, (f) his frequency of homosexual sex.

5. *Additional information.* Encounters with the police, appear-ances in court, respondent's age when this occurred; consultation with professional people about his homosexuality.

Thus, in addition to sample selection and the degree to which the samples were similar on demographic variables, the informa-tion from this questionnaire also enabled us to compare retro-spectively both experimental and control groups at time 1 insofar as their homosexual careers were concerned.

THE INTERVIEW

The interview was divided into two main parts: the first was designed to discover what typifications the respondent uses to organize his experiences and the manner in which they form the basis of his interpretations; and the second, his account and interpretation of the time spent in military service. Both parts were relatively unstructured; the first more so than the second. The first part of the interview was designed to get at the underly-ing presuppositions or "taken-for-granted's" held by the respon-dent. Thus, the questions asked were of a general nature in order to avoid suggesting any possible answers, or things that were "important," or any specific frame of reference to him. He would thus be forced to draw on his own stock of knowledge, rules of interpretation, and methods of accountability in answering. In-deed, interviewers were instructed not to answer questions such as "What do you mean by . . . ?" but to persuade the respondent to answer to the best of his ability.[3]

This was the opening ploy for each question. Certain probes were also provided which the interviewer used to follow up the initial answer to the question: (a) probes to ensure that the respondent did in fact answer the question; that is, to ensure that the respondent's typification scheme was presented; (b) probes

---

[3] We were guided in our interviewing techniques by Cicourel's work. See Aaron V. Cicourel, *Method and Measurement in Sociology* (New York: Free Press, 1964).

involving questions such as "What do you mean by that?," "Why is that?," "Why do you think that?," "What happened?," "Why did you do that?," "Can you give me an example from your experience?" These were designed to reveal the bases of interpretation used by the respondent in organizing his subjective world.

The sets of questions asked in the first part (Part I) of the interview were designed to reflect the theoretical categories of typification of self and typification of others. The second part (Part II) of the interview dealt directly with military service. All respondents were asked about:

1. Background variables: age of entry, voluntary enlistment or drafted, pay grade or rank.
2. Sexual experiences: sexual behavior while in service—who with, how often, where, how often compared to preservice. Finally, whether they thought their military experiences did anything to affect their homosexuality.
3. Other questions: did they ever get into any trouble while in the military, and whether they enjoyed their military service.

For those who received less than honorable discharges, a further set of questions was asked:

4. How they came to the attention of the authorities.
5. How their case was processed.
6. How getting this discharge has affected their lives.

The specific questions asked in Part I of the interview, and how they relate to the theoretical concepts employed, can be found in Appendix 2. The specific form of the questions used in Part II of the interview are found in Appendix 3.

QUESTIONNAIRE 2

After the interview, Questionnaire 2 was handed to the respondent to complete. Originally it was decided to collect all time 2 information by interview; however, this decision was altered to include a questionnaire as well. Some information was easier to obtain by a person checking a questionnaire, and the pretest of the interview showed it to be lengthy enough so that the inclusion of certain items on a questionnaire would reduce the time involved.

Questionnaire 2 included the following sets of questions:

1. Occupational history and problems at work.
2. Who knows or suspects respondent is homosexual.
3. Whose opinions are valued.
4. Number of friends and number of close friends.
5. The same questions asked in Questionnaire 1 on their homosexual careers, but this time worded "at the present time" rather than "at the time of your induction."
6. Questions on homosexual acculturation—ever having gone in "drag," ever lived with another homosexual, frequency of visiting "gay" bars.
7. Heterosexual experiences.
8. Religious behavior.
9. Political behavior (including homophile movement).
10. Items tapping psychological adjustment.

Questionnaire 2 served primarily to get at a person's objective experiences, that is, "Have you ever . . . ," "How many times have you . . ." (For the specific form of the questions see Appendix 4.)

All instruments were pretested, using respondents from the control "pool" who were not selected for the control group. (Unfortunately the questions for experimental group respondents on Part II of the interview were not pretested owing to the lack of sufficient members in this group.) After changes in the phrasing of some of the questions, the other main result of the pretest was to weed out some questions from the interview, some of which were discarded because they were redundant, and some which were converted into items on Questionnaire 2. This was mainly due to the fact that to complete the interview adequately took over three hours. This affected both interviewer and respondent; thus the time was shortened so that the whole interview (including the questionnaire) averaged out to about two and a half hours in length. The control "pool" was also used to train interviewers.

ANALYSIS OF DATA

The data were coded and put on IBM cards. Most of the questionnaire items were precoded so as to be taken straight off; codes were also established for the questions that appeared on the interview. Although every effort was made not to impose our own frame of reference on the interview data (especially Part I), it had been decided to subject these to statistical analysis. Thus codes were developed for replies to these nondirective questions. The following difficulties were faced:

1. Not all respondents mentioned items that reflected matters of theoretical concern.

2. Because the questions were nondirective, a great range of answers were given. This led to the development, in some cases, of very elaborate codes which, with a small N, made statistical comparisons difficult.

3. A preponderance of short answers in some cases—long pauses, "I don't know's," "I haven't thought about that." These should not necessarily be defined as "bad data." We recognize that what we assumed to be relevant to respondents need not in fact be so. Thus an "I don't know" or "I haven't thought about that" could indicate that the item referred to something that was not relevant for the respondent. The same phenomena can appear when a "cookbook" reply is given to a question for reasons of "something to say" or so as not to appear ignorant. This is not to say that such replies to a probe do not reveal "background features" or "taken-for-granted's," but they can be confounded by the sociology of the interview.

Developing a code for the interview, therefore, had its difficulties. The procedure adopted in constructing the code was to read over every interview before coding began. This enabled us to isolate patterns in the responses which acted as a guide in drawing up a code.

With regard to data analysis, the general form was to compare both groups on the "dependent" variable indicants and examine the consistency of the results obtained. Such differences were to be attributed to the effect of the so-called "independent" variable. This form of analysis, plus the nature of the data, determined what statistics were employed. Because most of the data were analyzed to produce frequencies in discrete categories and the measurement level involved was nominal or ordinal, Chi Square, Fisher's Exact Test, gamma, and z were used.[4]

In deciding upon levels of significance, Skipper et al. recommend that researchers state "the actual level of significance of each research finding" and let the reader determine its significance to him rather than selecting from one of the "sacred" levels.[5] They do, however, suggest that an opinion "regarding support or non-support of the data for the relevant hypothesis *may* be made by the researcher." While in sympathy with many of their criticisms, Labowitz provides certain criteria for selecting levels rather than automatically choosing .05 or .01.[6] We decided to report all levels of significance but, following Labowitz's suggestions, to use the .05 level as a guide; a more stringent level we felt was unnecessary because of the size of the sample and the type of tests employed. A less stringent level was unjustified because we were testing rather than developing hypotheses. When the direction of difference is predicted and appears, one-tailed probabilities are cited. In cases where a third variable was introduced for multivariate analyses, use was made of Goodman's method for analyzing three-factor interaction in contingency tables.[7]

4 For a description of z as a test for the significance of gamma, see Linton C. Freeman, *Elementary Applied Statistics: For Students in Behavioral Science* (New York: Wiley, 1965).

5 James K. Skipper, Anthony L. Guenther, and Gilbert Nass, "The Sacredness of .05: A Note Concerning the Uses of Statistical Levels of Significance in Social Science," *American Sociologist*, 2 (February 1967), 16–19.

6 Sanford Labowitz, "Criteria for Selecting a Significance Level: A Note on the Sacredness of .05," *American Sociologist*, 3 (August 1968), 220–22.

7 Leo Goodman, "Simple Methods for Analyzing Three Factor Interaction in Contingency Tables," *Journal of the American Statistical Association*, 59 (June 1964), 319–52.

Chapter 6

CHARACTERISTICS OF THE SAMPLES

The face data from Questionnaire 1 not only give us some indication of the social range of respondents in our sample, but also allows us to see if one of our groups differs from the other in any way as to make interpretation of our results problematic. (Not all the data from Questionnaire 1 will be presented —only those data which normally describe the parameters of a sample. Data on military characteristics of the sample come from the interview.) Where possible, these data will be compared to the Chicago study and to two other studies of homosexuals which used homophile organizations as their major sample source—a larger study by Weinberg and Williams where almost 90 percent of the sample came from M.S.N.Y., S.I.R., or Mattachine Society of San Francisco,[1] and Sagarin's study of M.S.N.Y.[2]

In the presentation of our data, rather than calling our groups experimental or control, or less than honorably discharged and honorably discharged, we use the convention, HD, to refer to

---

[1] Martin S. Weinberg and Colin J. Williams, *The Male Homosexual: A Cross-Cultural Study in Psycho-Sociology* (in progress). The larger Weinberg and Williams study included members of Mattachine and those on the mailing list (Mattachine of New York and San Francisco) as well as members of the San Francisco homophile society (S.I.R.). In addition, other homosexuals were obtained from bars and private clubs. The total U.S. sample was 1117.

[2] Edward Sagarin, "Structure and Ideology in an Association of Deviants," Unpublished Ph.D. dissertation, New York University, 1966. Sagarin divided his sample into members of Mattachine, subscribers (those on the mailing list, not necessarily members), ex-members, and friends. The last two categories will not concern us. His final sample included 192 members and 85 subscribers. As regards the characteristics of these two groups when compared, he says: "In general, the nonjoining supporters of Mattachine differ from the joiners in only a few ways; in most respects they are part of one population." (*Ibid.*, p. 172.)

those homosexuals honorably discharged from the military, and LHD, for those homosexuals whose discharge was less than honorable. Our data are presented first, followed, where relevant and possible, by data from the larger Weinberg and Williams and Sagarin studies. Finally, the characteristics of the Chicago sample are described.

AGE

There are no significant differences between our groups as regards age. As can be seen from Table 14, the majority in both

Table 14. Age Distribution, by Discharge Status

AGE	HD (N = 32)	LHD (N = 31)
Under 21	3%	0%
21–30	25	19
31–40	31	41
41–50	31	29
51 and over	9	3

When frequencies are combined in rows 1–3 and 4–5, $\gamma = -.04$, $z = -0.101$, two-tailed $p = .920$.

groups fall between age thirty-one and fifty. The corresponding figures (rounded) for Weinberg and Williams and Sagarin appear in Table 14A.

Table 14A. Age Distribution of Weinberg and Williams' and Sagarin's Samples

AGE	WEINBERG AND WILLIAMS (N = 1,039)	SAGARIN* (N = 191)
Under 21	4%	0%
21–30	28	29
31–40	31	29
41–50	21	24
51 and over	15	18

* Data collapsed to allow comparisons (Mattachine members).

These data are generally consistent with the present study and show that homophile members are distributed through all age categories but concentrate in the twenties and thirties. We are assuming that Weinberg and Williams' and Sagarin's studies accurately depict the age distribution of homophile members. This is not held with too great a conviction, however, as Weinberg and Williams' response rate was 30 percent and Sagarin's 61.5 percent for members and 55 percent for subscribers. No information is available for the nonrespondents in either study.

The distribution of the Chicago sample is shown in Table 14B.

Table 14B. Age Distribution, by Discharge Status (Chicago Sample)

AGE	HD (N = 48)	LHD (N = 32)
Under 21	0%	0%
21–30	46	56
31–40	40	37
41–50	13	6
51 and over	2	0

When frequencies are combined in rows 1–2 and 3–5, $\gamma = .20$, $z = 0.907$, two-tailed $p = .364$.

It will be remembered that the sample was constructed so as to eliminate an original age difference that appeared, using the total sample. Thus no significant difference in age appears between LHD and HD groups in the final sample of Chicago respondents. Also, as in the previous sample sources, respondents are concentrated in the twenties and thirties.

EDUCATION

As Table 15 shows, there are no great differences in education between our groups; in general, both groups are better educated than the population at large, with around 80 percent having received at least some college. This compares with Weinberg and Williams' data and those of Sagarin. Eighty-two percent of Weinberg and Williams' respondents had completed at least

Table 15. Education, by Discharge Status

EDUCATIONAL LEVEL COMPLETED	HD (N = 32)	LHD (N = 31)
8th grade or less	0%	0%
Some high school	3	3
High school diploma	9	23
Some college	34	29
College degree	37	19
Graduate degree	16	26

When frequencies are combined in rows 1–3 and 4–5, $\gamma = -.16$, $z = 0.377$, two-tailed $p = .706$.

some college, whereas Sagarin reports that of 195 Mattachine members, 158 (81 percent) have had or are now completing a college education. These figures are consistent with the data of the present study.

The data for the Chicago sample appear in Table 15A. Again, the sample was selected so as to eliminate a difference in education which appeared when the total sample was used. Thus, no

Table 15A. Education, by Discharge Status (Chicago Sample)

EDUCATION LEVEL COMPLETED	HD (N = 48)	LHD (N = 32)
8th grade or less	4%	9%
Some high school	4	6
High school diploma	11	11
Some college	40	34
College degree	4	3
Graduate degree	4	3

When frequencies are combined in rows 1–3 and 4–6, $\gamma = .15$, $z = 0.344$, two-tailed $p = .730$.

significant difference in educational attainment appears between the groups. Educational attainment of the Chicago sample appears lower than our previous sample sources, however, with only 45 percent of the total sample having received at least some college.

INCOME

As Table 16 shows, there is no great difference between our

Table 16. Income Distribution, by Discharge Status

TOTAL INCOME (last year)	HD (N = 32)	LHD (N = 31)
Less than $3,000	3%	3%
$3,000–$4,999	9	10
$5,000–$7,999	37	35
$8,000–$9,999	22	16
$10,000–$14,999	22	26
$15,000–$24,999	3	6
$25,000–$49,999	0	3
$50,000 and over	3	0

When frequencies are combined in rows 1–3 and 4–8, $\gamma = .03$, $z = -0.123$, two-tailed $p = .902$.

groups in income, with the median income falling between $5000 and $7999 per year. This seems low as compared to the educational level of the sample, with approximately 60 percent earning less than $10,000 a year. Most members of Weinberg and Williams' sample fell within the $5000 to $7999 category (31 percent), with approximately 67 percent of this sample making under $10,000 per year. The median income of Sagarin's sample of Mattachine members was $6550.

The Chicago data appear in Table 16A. Though the categories

Table 16A. Income Distribution, by Discharge Status
(Chicago Sample)

TOTAL INCOME 1966	HD (N = 48)	LHD (N = 32)
0–$2,999	10%	6%
$3,000–$4,999	2	9
$5,000–$7,499	35	41
$7,500–$9,999	23	19
$10,000–$14,999	25	19
$15,000 and over	4	6

When frequencies are combined in rows 1–3 and 4–6, $\gamma = .16$, $z = 0.725$, two-tailed $p = .468$.

are not entirely comparable, there is little difference from our other data, median income for the sample falling between $5000 and $7499 per year, with 73 percent of the sample earning under $10,000 a year. No significant difference appears between the HD and LHD groups.

OCCUPATIONAL LEVEL

Using Hollingshead's categories, the occupations of our two groups distributed as shown in Table 17.

Table 17. Occupational Level, by Discharge Status

OCCUPATIONAL LEVEL	HD (N = 32)	LHD (N = 31)
(1) Higher executives, major professionals, proprietors of large concerns	9%	10%
(2) Business managers, lesser professionals, proprietors of medium-size businesses	19	13
(3) Administrative personnel, minor professionals, small independent businesses	37	29
(4) Clerical and sales technicians	25	39
(5) Skilled manual employees	6	10
(6) Semiskilled and machine operators	3	0
(7) Unskilled employees	0	0

When frequencies are combined in rows 1–3 and 4–7, $\gamma = .28$, $z = 0.736$, two-tailed $p = .462$.

Again there is little difference between the groups, the majority of respondents falling into levels 3 and 4. There is a slight trend, however, for the HD group to more likely occupy the highest positions. Nearly 60 percent of our sample occupy one of the top three positions, which is a slightly lower percentage than Weinberg and Williams' sample (71 percent). Sagarin reports no data on occupational levels that are comparable, but states that his distributions indicate "a professional membership in the lower middle class economic group, having only limited financial success, and a white collar group (nonprofessional) having less economic success."[3] This is similar to categories 3 and 4 which account for the majority of our sample.

Again, though the categories used in the Chicago sample are not exactly the same, no significant difference appears between the HD and LHD groups (Table 17A). The data also show mem-

**Table 17A. Occupational Level, by Discharge Status
(Chicago Sample)**

OCCUPATIONAL LEVEL	HD (N = 48)	LHD (N = 32)
(1) Professional and Managerial I	0%	0%
(2) Professional and Managerial II	25	25
(3) Semiprofessional and Small Business	31	34
(4) Skilled Occupations	31	16
(5) Semiskilled Occupations	10	16
(6) Unskilled Occupations	2	9

When frequencies are combined in rows 1–3 and 4–6, $\gamma = .06$, $z = -0.275$, two-tailed $p = .784$.

bers of this sample as being in the higher levels of occupational prestige, 58 percent of the sample occupying one of the top three levels.

RELIGIOUS BACKGROUND

Table 18 shows the religious background of the majority of our

Table 18. Religious Background, by Discharge Status

RELIGIOUS BACKGROUND	HD (N = 32)	LHD (N = 31)
Protestant	59%	64%
Catholic	31	19
Jewish	0	13
Other	6	0
None	3	3

Combining rows 3–5, $df = 2$, $x^2 = 1.545$, two-tailed $p = <.50$.

---

[3] *Ibid.*, p. 109.

sample to be Protestant; there is no significant difference between the HD and LHD groups. Weinberg and Williams' sample included 53 percent Protestant, 29 percent Catholic, 9 percent Jewish, and 5 percent Other. The figures for Sagarin's sample of Mattachine members were 37 percent Protestant, 11 percent Catholic, 13 percent Jewish, and 38 percent Other, most of which he says are synonymous with None. Sagarin's figures are discrepant because he asked current religious affiliation rather than religious background. When we look at his data for parents' religion, we get 49 percent Protestant, 17 percent Catholic, 17 percent Jewish, and 15 percent Other, which is more consistent with our results.

The data for the Chicago sample which refers to the respondent's current religious preference show a similarity to Sagarin's data, with 46 percent (37) saying they were Protestant, 14 percent (11) Catholic, and 8 percent (6) Jewish. One percent (1) said Other, and 31 percent (25) None. There is no significant difference between HD and LHD groups. Looking at the respondent's father's religious background, 59 percent were Protestant, 15 percent Catholic, 9 percent Jewish, and 17 percent None. No significant difference appeared between HD and LHD groups.

RACE

There was only one black in our sample, in the San Francisco LHD group. Both Weinberg and Williams and Sagarin report very few blacks in their samples; Weinberg and Williams received replies from 39 blacks, Sagarin from 5. Blacks were excluded from the Chicago sampling.

SEXUAL ORIENTATION

Using a seven-point Kinsey-type scale, the sexual orientation of our groups were as shown in Table 19.

The percentages between the HD and LHD groups are very similar, with no significant differences appearing. Weinberg and Williams' and Sagarin's data are shown in Table 19A.

Table 19. Sexual Orientation, by Discharge Status

SEXUAL ORIENTATION LEVEL	HD (N = 32)	LHD (N = 31)
(0) Exclusively heterosexual	0%	0%
(1) Mainly heterosexual and insignificantly homosexual	0	0
(2) Mainly heterosexual and significantly homosexual	0	0
(3) Equally homosexual and heterosexual	3	6
(4) Mainly homosexual and significantly heterosexual	6	6
(5) Mainly homosexual and insignificantly heterosexual	28	19
(6) Exclusively homosexual	63	68

When frequencies are combined in rows 1–6, $\gamma = -.11$, $z = 0.171$, two-tailed $p = .864$.

Table 19A. Sexual Orientation Level: Weinberg and Williams' and Sagarin's Samples

SEXUAL ORIENTATION LEVEL	WEINBERG AND WILLIAMS* (N = 1,031)	SAGARIN† (N = 191)
(0)	0%	1%
(1)	0	1
(2)	2	0
(3)	4	3
(4)	13	7
(5)	30	28
(6)	51	60

* Replies were received from 46 heterosexuals also. These have been removed from this table.
† Table 2, p. 97, Mattachine members (amended).

From these data we can see that those who see themselves as either exclusively or near exclusively homosexual account for the majority of respondents.

In the Chicago study a majority of the respondents labeled themselves exclusively homosexual (Table 19B), though the size of the majority was smaller (50 percent) than for our sample (65 percent). No significant difference appears between the HD and LHD groups.

Table 19B. Sexual Orientation, by Discharge Status (Chicago Sample)

SEXUAL ORIENTATION LEVEL	HD (N = 48)	LHD (N = 32)
(0)	0%	0%
(1)	0	0
(2)	2	0
(3)	6	0
(4)	19	9
(5)	29	31
(6)	44	59

When frequencies are combined in rows 1–6, $\gamma = .31$, $z = 1.360$, two-tailed $p = .174$.

MILITARY BACKGROUND OF THE SAMPLES

In this section descriptions of the sample's military attributes are provided.

AGE AT INDUCTION

Table 20 shows the age at which members of our HD and

Table 20. Age at Induction into the Armed Forces, by Discharge Status

AGE AT INDUCTION	HD (N = 31)	LHD (N = 31)
Before 18	16%	19%
18–21	48	45
22–25	26	29
26–29	0	3
30 and over	3	3

When frequencies are combined in rows 1–2 and 3–5, $\gamma = .00$, $z = -0.263$, two-tailed $p = .792$.

LHD groups first entered the armed forces. As can be seen there are no great differences between the groups. When means were computed, the mean age of induction was 20.93 years for the HD group and 20.58 years for the LHD group. There is a difference, however, in the Chicago sample; as Table 20A shows, the LHD group entered the military at an earlier age than did the HD group. This difference is significant at better than the .04 level.

Table 20A. Age at Induction into the Armed Forces, by Discharge Status (Chicago Sample)

AGE AT INDUCTION	HD (N = 47)	LHD (N = 32)
Before 18	13%	34%
18–21	62	50
22–25	25	16
26–29	0	0
30 and over	0	0

When frequencies are combined in rows 2–5, $\gamma = .51$, $z = 2.063$, two-tailed $p = .040$.

BRANCH OF SERVICE

From Table 21 we see that for both groups the Navy was the

Table 21. Branch of Service, by Discharge Status

BRANCH OF SERVICE	HD (N = 32)	LHD (N = 31)
Army	19%	19%
Navy	47	45
Air Force	25	29
Marines	6	3
Coast Guard	3	3

A test of significance was not computed because the row categories are nominal and no large epsilon appeared to suggest a combination of cells.

most likely branch of service in which members of our sample served. There is no difference between the LHD and HD groups as to branch of service. A question on branch of service was not asked in the Chicago study.

PERIOD OF SERVICE

Regarding length of time served in the military, there is less of a difference than one might expect between our groups, as shown in Table 22. For example, while only 21 percent (7) of the HD group served less than two years compared to 33 percent (10) of the LHD group, there is virtually no difference between the

Table 22. Period of Service, by Discharge Status

PERIOD OF SERVICE	HD (N = 32)	LHD (N = 31)
6 months or less	0%	10%
7–12 months	3	3
1 year–18 months	9	10
18 months–2 years	9	10
2–3 years	25	16
3–4 years	28	16
4 years and over	25	35

When frequencies are combined in rows 1–4 and 5–7, $\gamma = -.26$, $z = 0.039$, two-tailed $p = .522$.

groups in the proportion of respondents who served for three years and over. The mean number of months spent in the military by the HD group is 43.5, whereas for the LHD group it is 52.2. This is confused by the LHD group including two or three long-term service people. When they are excluded, the average length of service for this group is reduced to 38.8 months. Nonetheless this does show that homosexuals can and do survive for long periods in the military without being discovered. A more marked difference appears between the groups in the Chicago sample (Table 22A). Forty-seven percent (15) of the LHD group had

Table 22A. Period of Service, by Discharge Status (Chicago Sample)

PERIOD OF SERVICE	HD (N = 48)	LHD (N = 32)
Less than 3 months	4%	19%
3–18 months	10	28
18 months–2 years	44	31
2–3 years	17	6
3–4 years	19	9
4 years and over	6	6

When frequencies are combined in rows 1–2 and 3–6, $\gamma = .67$, $z = 3.149$, two-tailed $p = .002$.

served for less than 18 months compared to 14 percent (7) of the HD group. This difference is significant at better than the .002 level.

TYPE OF DISCHARGE RECEIVED

Table 23 indicates the nature of the less than honorable dis-

Table 23. Type of Discharge Received—LHD Group

TYPE OF DISCHARGE	(N = 31)
General	39%
Undesirable*	55
Dishonorable	6

* Included here are servicemen who received Blue Discharges.

charge received by the LHD group. As can be seen, the majority of less than honorable discharges received are of the Undesirable type. No such data were provided by the Chicago study.

OTHER FACTORS

Two factors that might have affected the interpretation of our data were the proportion of officers in each group and the time of discharge for the LHD group.

Rank. Making inferences as to why the LHD group was discovered and the HD group was not, or on the effects of discharge, might be difficult if one group contained significantly more officers than the other. Both groups contained the same percentage of officers—19 percent. There were only two officers in the Chicago sample, both in the HD group.

Time of discharge. When a person is discharged is important, first, because military regulations change so that disposition of individuals for the same offense could vary at different times. Also, unofficial policies concerning "crackdowns" on homosexuals could operate at different times. There are slight differences among our groups concerning time of discharge, but these are not significant (Table 24). Of more importance is that within the LHD group, the majority (70 percent) of respondents received

Table 24. Time of Discharge, by Discharge Status

TIME OF DISCHARGE	HD (N = 32)	LHD (N = 30)
During World War II	16%	20%
1946–1950	25	7
1951–1961	34	47
After 1961	25	27

When frequencies are combined in rows 1–2 and 3–4, $\gamma = .31$, $z = 0.884$, two-tailed $p = .376$.

their discharges after 1951, when policy was more or less regularized, and few received them after 1961, which would, therefore, give long-term effects a chance to appear. No such data were provided in the Chicago study.

In conclusion, in terms of variables usually used to describe the parameters of a sample, our sample shows great similarity to those of Weinberg and Williams and Sagarin. Thus it appears unlikely that our respondents are atypical of respondents from homophile societies. We also found more similarities than differences when we compared our data with the Chicago sample comprising mainly nonhomophile organization members. There was a tendency for the Chicago sample to have less educational achievement, however. Neither in our sample nor the Chicago sample were significant differences found between the HD and LHD groups, eliminating a source of alternative hypotheses to any differences that may be found between these groups.

In comparing the military background of our sample with that of the Chicago sample, two differences appeared in the Chicago sample between HD and LHD group members that did not appear for our sample: the LHD group were more likely to have entered the military at an earlier age and to have remained in the military for a shorter duration than did members of the HD group.

Chapter 7

BEING DISCOVERED

The first research question we set for ourselves concerned the sociosexual factors that influence the probability of a homosexual being discovered by military authorities. As previously mentioned, our focus is on the contribution made by the deviant himself to his discovery.[1]

It will be remembered from Chapter 1 that two factors were considered to play an important role in the serviceman's discovery: (1) the frequency of his homosexual behavior prior to induction into the military, and (2) the nature of his homosexual conduct while in the military. With regard to this first factor, it was felt that those who frequently engaged in homosexual behavior prior to induction would be more likely to be discovered on account of their perception of the military situation in terms of homosexual opportunities. For the latter factor we anticipated a positive relationship between discovery and (a) frequency of homosexual sex while in the military and (b) the degree to which such sex was engaged in with other military personnel. Finally, it was decided to investigate the way in which these variables were associated with the manner in which the homosexual serviceman was discovered.

The results obtained were as follows:

MANNER OF DISCOVERY

The homosexuality of those respondents who were discovered came to the attention of military authorities in *three* main ways. Each is illustrated below.

---

[1] By "discovery" we mean those whose homosexuality was found out by military authorities and who received less than honorable discharges because of this. The possibility exists of the former occurring without the latter; e.g., receiving a separation with an Honorable Discharge or not being reported.

The most common manner of discovery involved *discovery through another person*. Seventeen of the respondents were discovered in this way (54 percent of the LHD group). This mode of discovery is sometimes related to jealousy, a lovers' tiff, or blackmail.

[R, a 28-year-old salesman, served in the Navy for almost three years before receiving an Undesirable Discharge. Exclusively homosexual before service.]

I was turned in by a civilian—he was a bartender. The ship came to Monterey and he fell in love with me. I couldn't stand him. . . . He said if I didn't become his lover he'd turn me in. I ignored him. He called ONI (Office of Naval Intelligence) and turned me in.

There were also cases where another serviceman was discovered and persuaded to reveal his previous sexual partners or who else he knew in the service to be homosexual. Through threats or promises or through a search of personal effects names are discovered.

[R, a 45-year-old policeman, served in both the Army and the Navy for a period of about six years receiving an Undesirable Discharge from each service. R exclusively homosexual before entering service.]

I was having an affair with a serviceman on a ship, who kept a diary. He was apprehended with another fellow and through this they got the diary and I was apprehended along with several other people.

This mode of discovery is often linked to many *voluntary admissions*—what we consider to be our second chief mode of discovery. To get out through voluntary admission, the military requires proof of homosexuality. The best proof is to provide the name of a partner who is also a serviceman. Not only can he be interrogated at length by military authorities, but there is the further possibility that he will supply additional names. Six of the seventeen cases who were discovered through another person were victims of servicemen who were one-time sexual partners and wished to get out of the service. An example of one such case is as follows:

[R, a 31-year-old male nurse. In the Navy seven years before receiving an Undesirable Discharge. No homosexual experience prior to service.]

A drag queen asked if "she" could stay in my apartment. I said yes, but don't hustle and don't bring tricks back. But she didn't listen to me. She brought two sailors back and we got into an orgy. They both wanted out of the service and used me as a reference. . . . I denied I was in the Navy but they went ahead and used my name.

Twenty-nine percent of the LHD group (9 cases) were voluntary admissions. The most frequent reason given for seeking discharge was dissatisfaction with military life. Generally absent from such accounts were any pressures that the homosexual might undergo, such as fear of exposure or the inability to control sexual tendencies. Such reasoning seems more an influence of stereotypical views of homosexuals, held especially by the military. Also of note is that few were unduly bothered by the potential stigma of a less than honorable discharge. Note the following case:

[R, a 50-year-old dress designer-manufacturer. Served in the Army for two and a half years before receiving an Undesirable Discharge. Exclusively homosexual before service.]

I felt I was just wasting time. . . . I wanted out because I was bored to death. . . . I had the advantage of being able to get out as a homosexual. . . . If I had been doing something of value I would have stayed.

The final manner of discovery was through the *homosexual's own indiscretion*. There were five cases (16 percent of the LHD group) where discovery was due to imprudent action on the part of the respondent.

[R, a 30-year-old hydraulic engineer. After serving two years in the Navy he was released with a General Discharge. No homosexual experience before service.]

It's not a very good story. I was turning gay and one feels he's the only one in that category. It was coming to the surface and I didn't want to control it and had sex and was caught in the locker room.

It is obvious from these cases that the homosexual serviceman runs a risk in engaging in homosexual behavior. Not only may he be directly discovered but there is even more of a chance of indirect discovery through being the "fall guy" in connection with another homosexual serviceman or through his name arising in connection with the other's case. No data on manner of discovery were provided in the Chicago study.

Having discussed the manner in which the homosexual serviceman is discovered, we turn to the factors we thought to be associated with the probability of discovery and whether these factors are related to the particular manner of discovery.

PRIOR HOMOSEXUAL FREQUENCY AND DISCHARGE STATUS

In an attempt to reconstruct the comparability of the HD and LHD groups when they entered the service the respondents were asked on the initial questionnaire how often they had been engaging in homosexual sex at the time of their induction. (We refer to this as "Prior Sex Frequency.") The results are shown in Table 25. The table shows that of those who before induction

Table 25. Discharge Status, by Frequency of
Homosexual Sex at Induction

| TYPE OF DISCHARGE | PRIOR SEX FREQUENCY | |
	High* (N = 16)	Low (N — 47)
LHD	69%	43%
HD	31	57

$\gamma = .50$, $z = 1.509$, one-tailed $p = .066$.
* Once a week or more.

were having homosexual sex once a week or more, 69 percent received less than honorable discharges. Of those who were having homosexual sex less than once a week, 43 percent received less than honorable discharges. This 26 percent difference is significant at the one-tailed .066 level (gamma = .50).

Other data regarding the stage of the respondent's homosexual career at the time of induction support the conclusion that those who eventually received less than honorable discharges were more likely to be further advanced than were those who eventually received honorable discharges. The supportive data include the following: the gamma between less than honorable discharge and associating with other homosexuals was .34, and the gamma between less than honorable discharge and extent of homosexual social activity was .34.

The Chicago study did not ask about sexual behavior (per se) prior to induction. It did include a question, however, which asked, "Did you begin to consider yourself homosexual before, during, or after your service in the Armed Forces?" Results of both studies are, therefore, not strictly comparable; that is, one can consider oneself homosexual without engaging in homosexual behavior, and vice versa. The results from the Chicago study are shown in Table 25A.

Table 25A. Discharge Status, by Perception of Self as Homosexual at Induction (Chicago Study)

TYPE OF DISCHARGE	CONSIDERED SELF HOMOSEXUAL BEFORE INDUCTION (N = 53)	DID NOT CONSIDER SELF HOMOSEXUAL BEFORE INDUCTION (N = 27)
LHD	43%	33%
HD	57	67

$\gamma = .21$, $z = 0.863$, one-tailed $p = .194$.

While in the same direction as our data, no significant difference was found between the LHD and HD groups insofar as self-perception as homosexual prior to induction is concerned.

SEXUAL BEHAVIOR IN THE MILITARY AND DISCHARGE STATUS

Our data suggest that there was a difference in sexual status between the LHD and HD groups at induction (although a high level of statistical significance is not obtained). We now consider whether there was a difference as regards homosexual behavior while in the military.

FREQUENCY OF SEX

Table 26 shows that of those engaging in homosexual sex more

**Table 26. Discharge Status, by Frequency of Homosexual
Sex in the Military**

| | FREQUENCY OF HOMOSEXUAL ACTS IN MILITARY | |
TYPE OF DISCHARGE	High* (N = 31)	Low (N = 32)
LHD	61%	38%
HD	39	62

$\gamma - .45, z = 1.624$, one-tailed $p = .052$.
* Once a month or more. Since this was in response to an open-end
interview question, the nature of the replies precluded more
precise categories than "at least once a month" or "less."

frequently, 61 percent received less than honorable discharges.
Of those engaging in homosexual sex less frequently, 38 percent
received less than honorable discharges. This 23 percent difference is significant at the one-tailed .052 level (gamma = .45). No
comparable item was included in the Chicago study.

TYPE OF PARTNER

With regard to sexual partners, respondents were asked
whether they had sex predominantly with military personnel
while they were in the forces. The results are shown in Table 27.

**Table 27. Discharge Status, by Usual Type
of Sex Partner**

| | USUAL PARTNER | |
TYPE OF DISCHARGE	Military (N = 22)	Not Military (N = 26)
LHD	82%	35%
HD	18	65

$\gamma = .79, z = 2.961$, one-tailed $p = .002$.
The decreased total N is due to those cases who did not have
homosexual sex while in the service.

Of those who engaged in homosexual sex predominantly with
other servicemen, 82 percent received less than honorable dis-

charges. Of those who did not have predominantly military
partners, 35 percent received less than honorable discharges. This
47 percent difference is significant at the one-tailed .002 level
(gamma = .79).

The Chicago study also asked who the usual type of sexual
partner was (Table 27A). Fifty-four percent of those persons

Table 27A. Discharge Status, by Usual Type of Sex
Partner (Chicago Study)

| TYPE OF DISCHARGE | USUAL PARTNER | |
	Military (N = 22)	Not Military (N = 42)
LHD	54%	31%
HD	45	69

$\gamma = .45$, $z = 1.823$, one-tailed $p = .034$.
The decreased total N is due to those cases who did not have homosexual sex while in the service.

whose partners were mainly other servicemen received less than
honorable discharges compared to 31 percent of those whose
partners were not mainly service personnel. This finding supports
our own—that those whose partners are mainly service personnel
run more risk of getting a less than honorable discharge than
those whose partners are not usually other servicemen.

In summary, we have seen thus far that not only are those who
have more frequent homosexual sex before they enter the military
less likely to receive Honorable Discharges, but that those who
have more homosexual sex while in the military and who restrict
this sex mostly to other servicemen are also less likely to receive
Honorable Discharges. This latter finding is supported by the
Chicago replication.

There is thus a relationship between discharge status and the
character of the respondent's homosexual career at induction as
well as his sexual behavior in the military. The question now can
be raised as to whether there is an interaction between these
factors in increasing the probability of less than honorable dis-

charge. To examine this, prior sex frequency was held constant, and discharge status was again run by in-service sexual frequency and type of sex partner. Goodman's test showed no significant interactions.

So far, therefore, the data support our hypotheses regarding factors involved in the probability of discovery. These relationships, which appear quite straightforward, turned out, however, to be more complex when the *manner of discovery* was considered. (As questions on manner of discovery were not asked in the Chicago study, replication of these results is not possible.)

PRIOR SEX FREQUENCY AND MANNER OF DISCOVERY

Among those who received less than honorable discharges, what is the relationship between their homosexual frequency at induction and the manner of their discovery? Table 28 shows the

Table 28. Manner of Discovery, by Frequency of Homosexual Sex at Induction

	PRIOR SEX FREQUENCY	
MANNER OF DISCOVERY	High (N = 11)	Low (N = 20)
Discovered through another person	55%	55%
Voluntarily admitted	36	25
Caught through indiscretion	9	20

The difference between rows 2 and 3 provides a two-tailed Fisher's Exact $p = .628$.

following: those who had higher frequencies at induction were more likely to come to the attention of military authorities by their own wish; those who were lower in frequency at induction were more likely to come to the attention of the authorities by being caught through their own indiscretion. Sexual frequency at induction was not related to discovery through another person; and the differences in the former categories have a two-tailed p of only .628.

SEX BEHAVIOR IN THE MILITARY AND
MANNER OF DISCOVERY

SEXUAL FREQUENCY IN THE MILITARY

Table 29 relates the frequency of in-service sexual behavior to

Table 29. Manner of Discovery, by Frequency of Homosexual
Sex in the Military

| MANNER OF DISCOVERY | FREQUENCY OF HOMOSEXUAL ACTS IN MILITARY | |
	High (N = 19)	Low (N = 12)
Discovered through another person	73%	24%
Voluntarily admitted	21	42
Caught through indiscretion	5	33

When frequencies are combined in rows 2 and 3, the difference between
extent of homosexual activity and whether or not respondents were
discovered through others provides a two-tailed Fisher's Exact $p = .019$.

manner of discovery. The table shows that those whose in-service
activity was high were more likely to be discovered through
another person. Those whose sexual behavior in the military was
relatively infrequent were more likely to be caught through their
own indiscretion or to admit to their homosexuality voluntarily
(two-tailed $p = .019$).

USUAL TYPE OF SEX PARTNER WHILE IN THE MILITARY

Table 30 relates the usual type of sex partner to manner of

Table 30. Manner of Discovery by Usual Type
of Sex Partner

| MANNER OF DISCOVERY | USUAL PARTNER | |
	Military (N = 18)	Not Military (N = 9)
Discovered through another person	56%	78%
Voluntarily admitted	22	22
Caught through indiscretion	22	0

The difference between rows 1 and 3 provides a two-tailed Fisher's Exact
$p = .062$.

discovery. The table shows that those whose sexual partners were predominantly other servicemen were more likely to have been discovered through their own indiscretion, whereas those whose sexual partners were not predominantly other servicemen were more likely to have been turned in by another person (two-tailed $p = .062$).

It is evident that of all variables considered, sexual frequency while in the military shows the strongest relationship to *manner of discovery*. If we look at sexual frequency in the military as specified by these other variables in its relationship to manner of discovery, we obtain some interesting findings which lead us to conclude that there are three main patterns that lead to the discovery of homosexuals by military authorities.

Two groups of LHD respondents had low frequency of sex while in the military. The first of these are those homosexuals caught through their own indiscretion. Their low frequency of sex while in the military is at variance with a frequency-probability model of risk, which would suggest that those discovered in this way would be engaging most in the behavior. *All* such cases did, however, report that their frequency was greater than it had been prior to induction. As these respondents were *all* engaging in sex primarily with other military personnel, and were not high in sexual frequency *prior* to induction, it seems reasonable to say that their discovery was mainly due to inexperience in a deviant role; that is, their indiscretion was not due to the extensity of their behavior but to ignorance of, or disregard for, the safest ways in which to engage in the behavior.

The second group of respondents who had low frequency of sex while in the military provide us with another pattern of discovery. These were those respondents who voluntarily admitted their homosexuality. Contrary to the above group, they tended to score high on sex frequency prior to induction,[2] and were more catholic in their choice of partners while in the military. From the interviews it was apparent that their disclosure was motivated by

---

2 Also, all but one of the voluntary admissions had labeled themselves as homosexual before induction into the military.

a desire to leave the service, the stigma of the discharge not being the major concern. Being further advanced in their homosexual career at induction seems to have made them less afraid to use their homosexuality to get out of the service.

The final pattern of discovery involves those respondents who differ from the above by having high frequency of sex while in the military. This group was primarily discovered through another person. Nothing was specified by sexual frequency prior to induction and, as regards type of sex partner, they were represented somewhat less among those having sex primarily with other servicemen. This pattern of discovery was most common to our respondents and represents those who put themselves more at risk through high frequencies of so-called deviant behavior.

The data reveal the deviant's role in his discovery. On the part of those who voluntarily admit their deviance, this influence is directly seen; in this case the homosexual uses a self label to gain a social label that can serve him. For those whose discovery is not voluntary, discovery involves placing one's self more at risk by the frequency of the behavior and imprudent choice of sexual partners. With our respondents there were no cases of a "bum rap." All had engaged in a form of behavior proscribed by the organization in which they were involved.[3] With regard to our original hypotheses about the relationships between less than honorable discharge and sexual behavior within and prior to military service, it can be seen that the data become meaningful only after manner of discovery is taken into account.

The data suggest, therefore, that the official labeling was related to the "quality and quantity" of the respondent's acts. As such, labeling theorists should perhaps make more precise the

---

[3] This is not to say that "bum raps" do not occur. For a description of such cases see Louis Jolyon West and Albert J. Glass, "Sexual Behavior and the Military Law," in Ralph Slovenko (ed.), *Sexual Behavior and the Law* (Springfield, Ill.: Charles C Thomas, 1964), pp. 250–72.

[4] This is Becker's phrase, used to describe those who assume "that the underdog is always right and those in authority always wrong." See Howard S. Becker (ed.), *The Other Side: Perspectives on Deviance* (New York: Free Press, 1964), Introduction.

character of their "unconventional sentimentality."[4] Such a stance does not preclude a recognition of the deviant's role in his own plight; on the other hand, this need not imply the sociologist's endorsement of the policies or processes of control agencies.[5]

---

[5] Conversely, it should be mentioned that attributing a recognition of the role of control agencies in the labeling process by no means implies their moral condemnation.

Chapter 8

THE SUCCESSFUL APPLICATION OF
AN OFFICIAL LABEL

After a person has been accused of or discovered in any act or
condition suggestive of homosexuality, military authorities are
faced with the question, "Is this a homosexual case we have
before us and, if so, what type?" Their decision is based upon the
reports of the various service intelligence agencies, military psychiatrists, and evidence from board hearings when held. The
sequence of events that follow the case of a serviceman charged
with committing homosexual acts or suspected of homosexual
tendencies usually proceeds along the following lines.

INTERROGATION

How the accused is interrogated depends on whether he
voluntarily requested separation or whether he came to the attention of the authorities in an involuntary way.

VOLUNTARY ADMISSION OF HOMOSEXUALITY

Interrogation has one paramount aim: a confession from the
accused. In the case of those who voluntarily admit to homosexual acts or tendencies, examination of the accused is cursory,
confined to just "getting the facts down." There is an attempt by
the investigators to gather as many names of other homosexuals
in the military as they can because it is their mandate to control
homosexuality as far as possible. Those voluntarily admitting
their homosexuality, therefore, in general do not undergo extensive investigation and interrogation. Usually they appear before
the commanding officer and other legal officers and usually have
to see a psychiatrist. Most of this investigative work involves
finding out whether any homosexual offenses were committed

while in the military and with whom. The best proof is the names of previous sexual partners, though other evidence, such as the character of the person's record or the psychiatrist's report, is also considered. The following experiences are related by those who voluntarily admitted to being homosexual.

I sought the aid of a Catholic priest who wasn't available so I went to a rabbi who told me what to do. He directed me to see a general in a mental hygiene unit. It involved a series of questions delving into my problem—basically finding out if I had had any sex while in the service. I denied it because I hadn't. (*Did you see a psychiatrist?*) Yes—his main point was in finding out if I was homosexual and was telling the truth. (*What did he ask?*) Just my gay experiences and my life with my lover.

The psychiatrist was very nice to me but the Head Psychiatrist was severe and wanted to know if I'd committed overt acts and I said No—that's all they cared about.

I went on sick call and they agreed to admit me to the hospital. I had to write out a long history of my sexual life. Eventually I was court-martialed. There were people there who testified to my lack of interest in firing guns and the like. . . .

INTERROGATION WHERE DISCOVERY WAS NOT VOLUNTARY

It is a frequent complaint of homophile societies who counsel homosexuals that either through ignorance or despair many accused homosexuals unnecessarily receive less than honorable discharges. One reason for this is because they do not exercise their rights under the law, but instead waive them. As a Society for Individual Rights pamphlet states,

If you do not waive your rights, the burden of proof will rest with the prosecutor and you will be defended by legal counsel at your trial. . . . As a matter of fact, it is often difficult to obtain a conviction for homosexual acts because the specific evidence to prove guilt "beyond a reasonable doubt" is hard to obtain, because corroboration . . . must be presented, because witnesses are often reluctant to testify, and because laws prohibiting homosexual acts in private have in most jurisdictions become dead letters. . . . Hence, if you do not waive your rights and if you do not confess, you have a good chance of obtaining a general (or even an honorable) discharge and of having the charges brought against you dropped for lack of evidence.[1]

In our research we have no cases of people who demanded their rights and really made a fight of it. Nor do we know the extent of those who are charged with homosexuality but later have the charges dropped. Both kinds of cases do exist but are small compared to the general reaction of servicemen accused of homosexuality. What evidence we have supports the belief of homophile organizations that the majority of homosexuals discovered by the military do not make a fight of it and in effect allow themselves to be discharged without honor. In many cases little investigation is necessary. For example, these cases may involve persons who make sexual advances toward other service personnel and where the evidence centers on the statements of the injured party.

It occurred aboard ship . . . what I think happened was that I made an overt pass at someone, touching their genitals . . . and he reported it to a superior. . . . There was some sort of an investigation but it was mostly in identifying me. It was mainly someone coming to my division and asking me what my name was. There wasn't any real investigation.

I was stationed at an induction center in Baltimore and I tried to make one of the sailors on duty and he reported it. There was no investigation to my recollection.

Other cases involve more effort on the part of the investigating agency. This effort is directed toward gaining cooperation from the accused; an effort that is usually successful. We discuss these cases according to the reason the accused serviceman gave for cooperating.

To protect others. One motivation for cooperating with investigators is to protect others whose names might come up in the

---

[1] Society for Individual Rights, *The Armed Services and Homosexuality* (San Francisco: Society for Individual Rights, no date), unpaged.

course of a detailed investigation. All cases here involved the respondent being informed upon directly or indirectly, and most were aware of their rights yet did not exercise them.

I was a chief and the mess cooks were my charges. They were about sixteen or seventeen [years of age] and had nothing to do all day and I got sexually involved with them and they caught one of them, or he turned himself in, I'm not sure, but anyway he implicated me. I was called to the Federal Building in San Francisco: they told me if I signed a paper the investigation would drop. I felt I could prevent the boys from being investigated and I had friends in the area whom I didn't want questioned.

One of the reasons I gave a statement was that I didn't want to start an investigation. (*Why not?*) Mainly because I was tired of lying and didn't want my friends investigated. I didn't take anyone out of the Navy with me, which happens in lots of cases.

At first I denied the whole thing; then they took my address book with the names of my friends and the children [of other Air Force personnel on the base] and questioned them. The kids didn't say too much, no details. Then they gave this airman a lie detector test and found everything he said was true. O.S.I. said I would go before a court-martial but it would drag the children through court and their parents didn't know about it. Eventually I gave in, there was one boy I loved and I didn't want to get him in trouble. . . . I saw a civilian lawyer but I didn't want the publicity. I didn't want the kids hurt so I just gave in.

Threats and promises. This is the most common reason given by the homosexual for his decision to cooperate. He is removed from his daily duties and set apart. Often frightened and confused, he is subjected to threats or promises on the part of investigating authorities who often have little evidence to secure a conviction. Under such pressure he is often willing to sign anything to stop the harassment and so cooperates. The following cases illustrate the experiences of some of our subjects in such situations. It is also of interest that most of the persons in this category claimed that either they were not informed of their rights, were erroneously informed about them, or were intimidated into not exercising these rights by investigating personnel.

The O.N.I. searched both my lockers—they took away picture albums and correspondence. They questioned me for six or eight hours, two of them; one was harsh, one was nice. They threatened me about going to my home town, telling why I was being investigated, tell my family. . . . When they said they'd inform my mother and father I was scared and wanted to protect myself and my family. . . . I told them everything and signed papers.

The Security Agent accused me of homosexual activities and asked if I would like to see a legal officer. I said, "Yes." I walked to a full Captain—I was told he was a legal officer—and he advised me to admit I was a homosexual. I asked . . . what would be the consequences. . . . He told me . . . if I admitted being a homosexual I would be released from the service with no complications . . . he stated I should admit to being a homosexual. I returned to the [Security Agent's] office. . . . I said that I did want help and have wanted help for so many years. I asked what would happen if I admitted to being a homosexual. He explained . . . the three categories of homosexual. He said this [Class II] is the category you fall into. . . . He said no punishment would be taken against me. [R received an Undesirable Discharge.]

I was in a daze the whole time . . . they [C.I.D.] told me about my life all the way back to when I learned to walk—when I got home people told me investigators had talked to them. They promised me I'd get a General Discharge if I told them all my partners. They told me there were Communist activities in the camp and if I helped them out they'd give me the General Discharge. [R eventually received an Undesirable Discharge.]

I took a polygraph test. . . . I was given three hours of extensive interrogation and I admitted the act and was required to dictate a statement which was in effect written by the investigators—they phrased everything. . . . I signed it. I was threatened during the interview that if I didn't admit they would investigate at my job and my neighbors and they promised that if I gave them all the facts and signed the statement that I could resign without any prejudice. [R was a naval officer and was discharged under "Other Than Honorable" conditions, which is equivalent to the Undesirable Discharge received by enlisted men.]

Such threats and persuasions are usually enough to make the homosexual waive his rights and confess. The investigating authorities are tenacious, and in representing the situation to be other than it is, the accused often feels he has little alternative but to cooperate.

Cooperated because "thought best." This last category included cases who said that they were honest persons and could not lie or found it very difficult to lie.

[They asked] are you homosexual? Ill advisedly I told them Yes. When confronted with a direct question I find it difficult to lie and so said I was homosexual.

Under these circumstances cooperation was quite voluntary and no threats or promises were needed.

We found a substantial number of cases where a lawyer was offered *after* the interrogation. By this time the accused person had already confessed, so that the provision of a lawyer would do him little good.

I saw a chaplain and he said to tell the truth and the Judge Advocate of the base told me I could not get any legal advice until the investigation was complete. I found out now that's a lie.

I signed a statement for the O.S.I. I received notice of trial and was assigned a lawyer. He asked me [about cooperating] and he said, "You've already hung yourself." He said I was screwed.

We also found cases in which the lawyer assigned to the accused suggested that he cooperate and not make a fight of it.

They sent me to talk to a Navy lawyer and he said they've got the goods on you; you're better off to take the Undesirable Discharge and get out. If ever anyone had told me I could keep quiet I'm sure all of this would have been different.

I got me a military lawyer. I waived my right to appear before a board. He said he saw no point in me appearing before the board and stirring up a lot of trouble.

APPEARANCE BEFORE A PSYCHIATRIST

Approximately 71 percent (22) of our sample said that they had to see a psychiatrist during the investigation. Most found this to be of little personal help.

In a five-minute interview he said I was a compulsive neurotic. He asked did I wet the bed, bite my nails, have migraine headaches. I answered No to all, and he said I was sick.

I had a half-hour interview with a psychiatrist. All he said was how many children did I think you should have in an ideal family and I said four or five; he said "What are you?" and I said tenth. He said you may have an unconscious wish you were sorry you were born.

Our respondents may be embittered in their recollections; but contacts with a military psychiatrist almost preclude personal assistance for the homosexual, since the psychiatrist is on the "side" of the government. This places the psychiatrist in a medicoethical dilemma. As doctors they have a responsibility to their patients. At the same time, as officers in the military they have a responsibility and a duty to report all cases of suspected homosexuality. This creates a role conflict situation for military psychiatrists, a problem which has received extended discussion by them.[2]

It is a fact, however, that military law has not extended full protection to servicemen regarding the statements given to psychiatrists. Military psychiatrists generally do not warn the individual of his rights against self-incrimination, which results in a psychiatrist's testimony often being used to incriminate and convict homosexuals in court-martials. The law appears to be even less restrictive in the case of administrative proceedings

---

[2] Louis Jolyon West and Albert J. Glass, "Sexual Behavior and the Military Law," in Ralph Slovenko (ed.), *Sexual Behavior and the Law* (Springfield, Ill.: Charles C Thomas, 1965). Richard G. Druss, "Cases of Suspected Homosexuality Seen at an Army Mental Hygiene Consultation Service," *Psychiatric Quarterly*, 41 (January 1967). For a discussion of how such conflicts are handled see Arlene K. Daniels, "The Social Construction of Military Psychiatric Diagnoses," in Hans Peter Dreitzel (ed.), *Recent Sociology No. 2: Patterns of Communicative Behavior* (New York: Macmillan, 1970).

where the rules of admissibility of evidence are less demanding. A similar situation also seems to hold in the case of statements given to military chaplains.[3]

APPEARANCE BEFORE A BOARD

Most homosexual cases in the military are of the Class II type, which are dealt with administratively rather than by court-martial. Most persons accused of homosexuality do have the right and are informed that they may have their case heard by a board of officers. If the accused serviceman denies the charge against him, then an appearance before the board is necessary; if he admits the charge, then he has the option of going before the board or waiving that right and accepting whatever discharge they recommend. Even in admitting the charge, an appearance before a board can sometimes lead to a General, and even theoretically, an Honorable Discharge, depending on the circumstances of the case. The experience up to this point, however, is usually enough to produce a confession, waive the right to appear before a board, and accept an Undesirable Discharge. In our sample of those who had the opportunity to appear before a board of officers (27), some 81 percent (22) waived this right. This almost guaranteed them an Undesirable Discharge.[4]

The waiver of appearance before a board of officers seems to

---

[3] For a discussion of these points see Edward L. Sherman, "The Civilianization of Military Law," *Maine Law Review*, 22 (1970), 70–72.

[4] The question can be raised as to whether the individual knows the possible adverse consequences of a less than honorable discharge when he waives his right to a board hearing. The following is an example (from the Army) of what the individual signs when he waives his right. It was furnished us by one of our respondents.

> I further understand that if an Undesirable Discharge is issued to me that such discharge will be under conditions other than honorable; that as a result of such discharge I may be deprived of many or all rights as a veteran under both Federal and State laws and that I may expect to encounter substantial prejudice in civilian life in situations where the type of service rendered in any branch of the Armed Forces or the type of discharge received therefrom may have a bearing.

be the usual thing. Consider the following evidence given to the 1962 and 1966 Hearings.

ARMY

The only data the Army had on board action that was waived by homosexuals referred to the raw number of persons so deciding. It is thus impossible to tell what proportion of all such cases exercised such waivers. The data do show a steady increase in numbers from 111 in April 1959 to 571 in June 1964.[5] With regard to officers they provide the following data. Statistics for fiscal years 1962 through 1965 indicate 286 resignations in lieu of board action. Of this number, 210 (73 percent) received separations under other than honorable conditions.[6] Unfortunately, we do not know the corresponding proportion of such discharges for those who did appear before a board, so we cannot make any statement of the effects of appearing before a board on subsequent discharge status. In addition, this figure represents all types of cases, and not just those involving homosexuality.

NAVY

Data are offered for unfitness and misconduct discharges which would include some homosexuals. From a sampling of cases in 1961, three out of four such cases in the Navy exercised the waiver.[7] A sampling in 1965 showed the proportion to be 80 percent.[8] Specifically with regard to Undesirable Discharges, the Navy further states that 20 percent of "personnel processed for possible undesirable discharges requested a board hearing."[9] As the majority of homosexuals separated from the Navy do eventually get Undesirable Discharges, we suggest that approximately 80 percent waive their right to a board hearing. It could be higher or lower; we cannot say, as we are bracketing the question

---

[5] 1962 Subcommittee Hearings, p. 858; 1966 Subcommittee Hearings, p. 1037.
[6] 1966 Subcommittee Hearings, p. 1038.
[7] 1962 Subcommittee Hearings, p. 917.
[8] 1966 Subcommittee Hearings, p. 1028.
[9] *Ibid.*, p. 944.

of whether there is a relationship between what the individual processed for possible Undesirable Discharge is charged with and whether or not he waives his rights.

The information is as unclear insofar as officers are concerned. All we know is that from 1957 to 1965, 69 to 91 percent of officer separations involved resignations and waivers of board action.[10] As in the case of enlisted men, we do not know the number of homosexuals involved in these figures. In both cases also we do not know how the decisions to appear or not to appear before the board affected the discharge received.

It is from the Air Force that we get the most detailed information for our purposes. For 1961, statistics show that for cases involving homosexuals only about 15 percent of those involved requested a board hearing.[11] Furthermore, for the period July 1962–June 1965, 81 percent of those persons discharged for homosexuality waived board proceedings.[12] We are also able to see the relationship between waiver and discharge received, in Table 31.

Table 31. Administrative Discharges, Class II Homosexuals, Air Force Enlisted Personnel 1962–65

EVENTUAL DISCHARGE	BOARD HEARING	BOARD WAIVED
Honorable	121 (25%)	300 (18%)
General	224 (47%)	727 (36%)
Undesirable	133 (28%)	914 (46%)

SOURCE: 1966 Hearings, p. 967 (amended table).

From the data the Air Force provides, it appears that those homosexuals who elect to appear before a board are most likely to receive a General Discharge and have a more or less even chance of getting an Honorable or Undesirable Discharge. Those

---

10 *Ibid.*, p. 1028.
11 1962 Subcommittee Hearings, p. 951.
12 1966 Subcommittee Hearings, p. 969.

who waive their right, however, are most likely to get an Undesirable Discharge. Of those who chose a board appearance, 25
percent received Honorable Discharges compared with 18 percent of those who waived the right. Of those who chose a board
appearance, some 28 percent received Undesirable Discharges
compared with approximately 46 percent of those that waived
the right. We know nothing of the cases that chose one alternative or the other; it does seem probable, however, that choosing
not to appear before a board adversely affects the character of
the discharge received.

We have raised the question as to why the homosexual serviceman usually waives his right to a hearing, and find that there are
basically two answers. First are those instances where the individual wants to leave the service and uses his homosexuality as
an excuse. Second are those instances where discovery leads to
fear and confusion on the part of the accused individual, added
to which a thorough and often unfair interrogation feeds the
desire to stop the degradation as soon as possible. The position of
these latter cases has been adequately described as follows:

> Through one means or another an allegation is made that the man
> committed a homosexual act or manifests the existence of homosexual
> tendencies. The accusation is so repugnant to our society that I would
> venture to say that in 90 percent of the cases, the man, when con-
> fronted with the allegation . . . goes through a traumatic period
> where he just doesn't know what to do.
>
> He doesn't want to confide in his family or doesn't know who to
> turn to or what can be done. The only one logically he could routinely
> turn to would be his counsel. He is afraid of exposure to his family.
> He is afraid of exposure to his contemporaries. So the easy way out
> that is proposed to him is to sign a waiver.[13]

When the accused serviceman desires a hearing, a board is
convened. The operations of such boards and their weaknesses in
providing adequate safeguards to the serviceman accused of

---

[13] Statement made by Neil B. Kabatchnick, Chairman, Military Law Committee, the Bar Association of the District of Columbia, to the 1962
Subcommittee Hearings, p. 519.

homosexuality have been discussed in Chapter 2.[14] Few of our sample actually appeared before such boards; therefore no further discussion is offered.

DISPOSITION AND DETENTION

During the investigation and afterwards, the accused serviceman is socially segregated, and often spatially segregated from his fellows while awaiting separation. The variety of places and situations reported by our respondents are shown in Table 32.

Table 32. Place of Residence While Awaiting Discharge

PLACE	(N = 31)
Same unit, same duties	26%
Same unit, different duties	6
Discharge center	23
Hospital	26
Prison	16
Other	3

The majority of our respondents claimed they experienced little hardship while they waited for their discharge. Many kept to their original duties while under investigation. This was not the case for most naval personnel, however, who could not be kept aboard ship and who were usually sent to detention barracks. Naval brigs segregate homosexuals from other prisoners, which often makes the homosexual subject to intimidation and sexual exploitation. The following description of life in a naval prison comes from a Class I homosexual who not only was imprisoned prior to his trial but was sentenced to five years imprisonment for a homosexual offense. He served only nine months before rigorous efforts on the part of his family got him released and separated, but still with a Dishonorable Discharge.

---

[14] For other limitations in board proceedings and current congressional proposals for reform see Clifford A. Dougherty and Norman B. Lynch, "Administrative Discharge: Loophole in Military Justice?", *Trial*, 4 (February–March 1968), 19–21, and Norman B. Lynch, "The Administrative Discharge: Changes Needed?", *Maine Law Review*, 22 (1970), 141–69.

I waited three months in the brig [before trial—General Court-Martial]. . . . This trustee, who wasn't locked up, had some of the guys blowing him through the bars. . . . He wanted me to but I wouldn't . . . in the brig you had all kinds, murderers, embezzlers, AWOLS, rapists. . . . They kept the murderers manacled. I thought I'd go out of my mind. They were chained to the bars. Then one of the masters at arms, one guard, stuck it [his penis] through the bars. I didn't, I was afraid to. In the brig awaiting trial, when it got out I was homosexual, this Marine guard got on my back. He gave me a toothbrush—cleaning the deck in the men's room with a toothbrush.

I get my judgment, reduced to apprentice seaman [he had been in for three years, an enlisted man with the rank of Yeoman 2nd Class], jail for five years and Dishonorable Discharge. I was so depressed, I went back [to the brig] and cried. I thought of suicide, of hanging myself with a towel. . . . They shipped me in handcuffs to Portsmouth—an eerie place, like a castle, on a hill, like the moors, with fog. Oh! I was depressed. At this prison the receiver said, "Uh ha! Another blow job."

They put me in "Scan Row," Scandalous Conduct row, where they keep homosexuals separately. I was alone, we were all separated, no one to talk to. I said I'd never survive. My hair was cut down to the scalp and they gave you a label with your name on and charge and number of years—everyone looks at you and knows.

From April to June I worked in the laundry. I couldn't take the heat, I was still very suicidal. Then they put me in the sewing shop—I couldn't stand that, the machines, I couldn't take the noise. . . . We had calisthenics every day; you couldn't talk, only at recreation twice a week. But the Marines [guards] came in close to hear.

One night I'm lying in my bunk. I see my door opening; another sailor jumps right in. The trustee let him in. I had to let him do me —sodomy, anal intercourse, I had to let him. That's only the beginning [R was subject to other homosexual attempts, some he gave in to, others he was a willing partner]. . . . They'd all whistle at me.

This was the only case in our sample who received a prison sentence for homosexual behavior. Other persons who were put in naval establishments for a short time while awaiting discharge, however, did mention similar facets of the situation—the segregation from other prisoners and the contempt and intimidation faced from them and from guards. In general, however, members of our sample suffered little hardship pre- and post-investigation till their discharge. Twenty-one out of thirty (or 70 percent) said they were treated well by others during this period and that they were able to keep their situation concealed from their fellow servicemen.

One final point concerns the period of time from the beginning of the investigation to eventual discharge. For the whole sample, the mean length of time was 2.56 months, with the Navy representing the longest period (2.68 months). This is at variance with West et al. who, in a study of 141 homosexual cases awaiting discharge from the Air Force, found there was an average of five months from the time of completion of the investigators' report till the date of separation.[15] (For our Air Force personnel, the average was 1.8 months.) Why this difference should be so great we do not know. A possible answer lies in the differences between services. For a start, our sample was weighted heavily in favor of naval personnel. Second, because our number of Air Force cases are smaller, they are, in all likelihood, less representative of Air Force personnel processed for homosexuality than are those in West's sample. Our data are shown in Table 33.

Table 33. Length of Time from Beginning of Investigation to Eventual Discharge

LENGTH OF TIME	(N = 31)
Less than one month	26%
1–2 months	19
2–3 months	23
3–6 months	16
6 months and over	16

In conclusion, the manner in which military organizations process their deviant members is a function of the fact that they are able to operate under almost clandestine conditions. Investigations into the workings of military bureaucracy are interpreted

---

[15] Louis Jolyon West, William T. Doidge, and R. L. Williams, "An Approach to the Problems of Homosexuality in the Military Service," *American Journal of Psychiatry*, 115 (November 1958), 392–41.

as a threat to security, and criticisms of military activities are often considered "unpatriotic." Under these conditions the military establishes an autonomy of action that allows it great freedom to deal with its members as it thinks best. Despite the Uniform Code of Military Justice (1950) and more recent attempts to extend civil rights to servicemen, features of military organization still maintain it as one of the most "total" of total institutions in this society. It is possible, therefore, for it to deal swiftly and surely with any of its members who are defined as threats to good order and morale.

This is seen quite clearly in the case of those servicemen who are accused of homosexual conduct. The processing of such personnel is routinized in formal and informal ways so as to cause as few problems as possible for the organization. Suspects are processed so as to confess and thus avoid a hearing; the hearings themselves provide little protection to the accused. The system is arranged so that the homosexual serviceman is isolated, unprotected, and without the support of others. In the atmosphere created by his exposure he, in effect, discharges himself.

Chapter 9

INTERPRETING THE EFFECTS OF
THE OFFICIAL LABEL

INTERPRETATIONS OF OBJECTIVE EFFECTS

This chapter examines the way in which respondents interpreted the effects of a less than honorable discharge. We proceed by first examining respondents' answers to the question, "Has getting a less than honorable discharge affected your life at all?"

In answer to the above question, 18 out of 31 (or 58 percent) of the LIID group said getting such a discharge had affected their lives, while 13 (42 percent) said it had made very little or no difference. It was expected that those high in homosexual frequency prior to military service might claim that their discharge affected them less than those less advanced. Although we did find such a difference, as Table 34 shows, it was not large

**Table 34. Effect of Receiving a Less Than Honorable Discharge,
by Prior Sex Frequency**

DISCHARGE INTERPRETED AS HAVING AN EFFECT	PRIOR SEX FREQUENCY	
	High (N = 11)	Low (N = 20)
Yes	45%	65%
No	54	35

$\gamma = -.38$ $z = 0.066$, one-tailed $p = .474$.

enough to be considered statistically significant.

As to the nature of these effects, it is evident from the interviews that they were mainly economic, centering around the inability to obtain certain jobs and the fear of expulsion from jobs that were already held. It is also evident that for most respondents these problems were short-lived, and by a series of adjustments they were able to find employment that suited them and in which their success precluded dismissal should their discharge be discovered. A second main effect was more psychological in nature and represented the feelings about receiving such a discharge. These feelings mainly concerned the period shortly after the discharge and ranged from feelings of deep depression and shame to anger and disgust at the way they had been treated.

It is worthwhile to examine the evaluation of the effects of less than honorable discharge in more detail. Of those who said that their discharge had affected their lives, 10 (or 56 percent) remarked that the most important effect for them was in losing or being refused a job. Of the remaining 8, all mentioned that although they had never lost a job, they had been unwilling to try for the job of their choice because of the fear that their record would be thrown up to them. The following are examples of those who lost or were refused jobs because of their discharge.

[The discharge] affected my mental attitude toward myself—it put me on the defensive all my life. I've always been afraid that I'd be hurt again. I could never go through that again, I'd rather die. . . . I've lost some jobs. I'd fill out the papers and if they asked about your discharge I'd just leave. I had studied teletyping, I couldn't take those jobs. . . . I applied at a clothing store and wrote that I had an Undesirable Discharge. They asked what for and I told him [the manager]. He smiled and said he was sorry he couldn't help me. Since then I never tell anyone. I don't want to be hurt again.

I had a position before I went in [the Navy] and the employer had to take you back, but you had to have a good release. He [employer] refused to take me back because of my release. My family was supporting me; if it wasn't for them I'd have committed suicide. I got to drinking heavily—I couldn't find a job in my home city. You should see the places I'd go. By telling my original employer, he was telling others . . . it was the only reference I had.

It's very difficult to get a job. I had applied for a job at G.E. and I told them about my discharge. He said he could have hired me if I had served my time in prison for murder but not with that discharge. The . . . [department store] told me, we're sorry, we don't employ homosexuals. I tried to get a job with a trucking firm but they asked about the discharge. Wherever you go that discharge hangs over your head. Eventually it forced me into an occupation I hate.

For some persons, therefore, the period after discharge is often one of economic hardship. Regardless of qualifications, they find that they cannot operate in the labor market as other people or as they did before. For many this represents their full realization of what being "deviant" means.

Our other category, those who are afraid or unwilling to go for certain jobs, represents those who in the awareness of their deviant status attempt to avoid the pain and shame of being confronted with it in public.

My own doubts influenced my actions when I first got out [of the Army] in not going for interviews for jobs . . . it really gripes me because I'm working at a job which requires less qualifications than I have.

I couldn't take government jobs or police jobs, any jobs where they'll do any investigating of my background. I don't try for those. I don't want to be investigated. I don't want it made public.

The extreme position is represented by the following case:

I've never lost a job but I have felt forced to terminate a job for fear of being discovered. I've also not applied for many jobs because I knew they were defense contractors [and would require a security check].

In this category are those who are unable to follow occupations for which they are qualified either by experience or education. With increasing governmental involvement in private sectors of industry through, for example, defense contracts, as well as the fear of industrial espionage, many positions require a security check. Thus, it is extremely difficult if not impossible for the person who has received a less than honorable discharge to avoid being discovered by such firms. Such a possibility, therefore, excludes certain employment from these persons. In addition, of course, and for the same reasons, all federal and many state positions are closed to persons who are so discharged. This is very frustrating to those who have the technical and educational qualifications for such positions but are aware that they have been defined as lacking the requisite moral qualifications.

I was in cryptography and had access to all traffic in the service; I heard all communications from Russia. It was an extremely high security job. I could get a well-paying job now if I had an Honorable Discharge. This would require a security clearance. Since mine was taken away I know I would never get another one now. . . . I've never taken a job I knew would involve a background check.

The following case exhibits a similar phenomenon. It is also interesting in that it illustrates the secondary deviance that can ensue as a result of the employment difficulties following a less than honorable discharge.

I lost my security clearance and am unable to get one. My field was industrial health, radioactive stuff. . . . It requires a security clearance. [R was a hospital corpsman in the Navy.] Anyone that could use me has defense contracts and because they have defense contracts they can't use me. I applied for three or four jobs and they asked for my discharge and said, "Sorry, we can't use you." I took a job in a bookstore, then a sporting goods store, then unemployment, then I hustled on the street to supplement that. (*How soon was it before you got a permanent job?*) About eighteen months, as a night orderly in a hospital. . . . I wish I had the job I trained for.

Some of our respondents bluffed or took the chance that they would not be discovered. This created considerable tension for them, which usually was not worth it because often their discharge came to light. This was the situation of the following respondent.

First I couldn't get any kind of work I wanted. I had to take jobs that didn't require any investigation. I had to hide my Undesirable Discharge from the public. Eventually I got a job with . . . Aircraft in a classified area and they didn't investigate too far—I told them I wasn't in the service. After four years everyone in my section had to fill out a form for clearance . . . so I just quit. I knew I couldn't get the clearance because of my discharge.

The situation can also be difficult in occupations like the professions where discharge status is not a bar to entry. The following respondent is a neurosurgeon who maintains that advancement within his profession was retarded because of his discharge.

I finished medical school and had interned before the service. When I came out [of the Air Force with an Undesirable Discharge] ready for residence, the head of the department called me into his office and said he knew about my discharge. When I applied for final certifying boards he told the board that I was homosexual. I wasn't allowed to take certification. I wasn't certified until just now, ten years later. (*How do you know he told?*) I don't, but being the head of the department he had to report my background to the board. . . . I would have been able to get a better position in the same occupation if not for this discharge.

The final case we shall examine shows the disorganization that can occur in a person's life due to employment problems ensuing from a less than honorable discharge. In this case, the opposite of secondary deviance occurred, an attempt to be hyperconformist in order to maintain employment.

I applied for a federal job, General Service Administration [after discharge from the Navy], and was accepted on a temporary basis. No inquiry was necessary, and all was okay for a year. I took another job then, but this was terminated [labor cutback] so I went back to the federal job I had before. One day they said I was permanent and I had to sign papers. Then I got a call to go to the investigating office. They wanted me to explain the discharge and said I would be fired unless I appealed it. The boss suggested I go to an attorney. He asked if I was going with a girl and planned to marry. I had a girl friend and I went and asked her to marry me and she said Yes and the appeal was forwarded telling them of this. . . . I don't know why I did all this except to prove to the other people at the office that I wasn't homosexual. [The marriage] lasted two months. I did discover I was homosexual, so it was trickery on her for society's sake.

First of all the marriage split. . . . [Then] I was informed that I was to be relieved of my duties—terminated, with no appeal. I was jobless with a wife on my hands. [Then] my wife, to get even with me, had taken the credit cards and run up a bill of $8,000. At this time I got a letter from the Navy Department saying my discharge would not be changed. I lost all the way round. I went bankrupt and applied for a divorce. Unemployment supported me. I wasn't sure what I was or who I was. . . . I lived alone for about two years, I was rather erratic and drank heavily. [This happened about four years ago. Since then, he has paid off all his debts and lawyers' fees and is going to school studying electronics. He is doing quite well financially and reported that since then his discharge has had no effects on his life.]

In examining the thirteen cases who reported that their less than honorable discharges had no effects upon their lives, it is apparent that these persons obtained employment soon after they were discharged, or have had a series of jobs in which the question of discharge has never arisen. Prominent among this group are people whose occupations are professional or artistic, who do not work in large organizations or bureaucracies, and are not involved in anything having to do with security clearances. For example, among this group we have an artist, a professional musician, a free-lance journalist, a college professor, and an attorney; another seven are working in private industry. None claimed that his discharge has prevented him from pursuing the occupation of his choice or one for which he is qualified.

The important point seems to be getting a job within a short time after leaving the military; this seems to allay many fears concerning the effects of the discharge.

I went back home; there was apprehension, I was afraid, the unknown. Once I was released and got home and found life hadn't ended I picked up. It was no joke, I was serious about it. I saw there was no point in worrying about what had happened—the best thing to do was to pick up the pieces and start over again. The future did seem dim. I guess I overromanticized—I saw myself shining shoes or picking rags. I associated it with my discharge. I imagined I'd never be able to get a job and all sorts of ridiculous things. [R got a job without any trouble fairly soon after discharge.]

I thought it [the discharge] would [affect me] at first. I had a deep guilt complex, but when I got a job . . . and they didn't do any checking I thought what the hell. Before that I really did have a guilt complex.

The final case we consider among those who claimed that their discharge had not affected them shows the range of effects the discharge can have. We have seen how some respondents were greatly affected by their discharge. The following respondent claims he was not affected at all. He is of interest in that he received *two* Undesirable Discharges, one from the Army and one from the Navy, and now has a full-time position as a policeman and a part-time position as a minister.

(*Do they know you are homosexual at work?*) Some of the guys in my company have suspicions as I was carrying on with one of their boys. The Inspector I work under knows and the Sheriff—they've been to my home and I've been to theirs—it's an unspoken fact. The FBI confronted me and asked, "Are you or are you not a homosexual?" I said, "Absolutely," and I'm working on international security—they know about my military record. (*What did the FBI do?*) They thought I was bullshitting. (*Did anything happen after that?*) Nothing, it was a matter of record. (*Has your discharge affected you at all?*) Not to my knowledge it hasn't. (*What happened after your discharge from the Navy?*) [R was in underwater demolition.] I went down to the Army Recruiting Center and enlisted three months after I left the Navy. I left the discharge part blank [on the application form].

[R had been in the Navy four years and had reached the rank of Boatswain 1st Class before receiving an Undesirable Discharge. He was five and a half years in the Army reaching the rank of Sergeant before he again was separated with an Undesirable Discharge for homosexuality. In the Army he was in the Commandos.]

(*Did you have problems with either of your discharges after you left the service?*) No, I don't even have a copy of any of them. I trained to be a minister, and at college they asked for my discharge and I just said I served and they didn't ask further. I was an officer at the time, and a policeman is above and beyond reproach.

The effects of a less than honorable discharge, therefore, vary widely among our respondents. To some, it occasions complete collapse, depression, and difficulty with employment; to others, it seems to have little or no effect. For the majority who claim to have been affected, the effect centers predominantly on employment and seems to be of short duration. For most, there is a period of uncertainty after leaving the service, but, eventually, after certain adjustments, and especially after obtaining a permanent and satisfactory job, the experience becomes defined as not as crucial as they had once expected it to be. Most affected are those who are qualified by education or experience for occupations which they had intended to be careers and which now they cannot pursue. This involves a great loss of investment and often the misery of working at a job that does not satisfy them.

METHODS OF AVOIDING OBJECTIVE EFFECTS

We next examine some of the methods used by our respondents to nullify the potential effects of their discharge. The most common method used is one or another form of misrepresentation, of hiding the fact that they have been labeled as deviant by the military.

I have to lie to cover up. When they [employers] say "Service?" I say No and hope they don't check it out. Sometimes I have to lie and say, "Hardship case, I had to leave after thirty days." One job I leveled with the guy and said I was a homosexual. He said, "Between you and I this has no bearing, you're qualified." [But] he checked into company policy and apologized that they don't hire homosexuals; since then I lie.

I applied for a job and said I'd been discharged medically. I was accepted and they said bring in your discharge papers. I told them they had got lost and it takes six months to get them. They said show them to us when you get them. For the first year and a half I was afraid they'd remember and want to see them. (*Did they?*) No.

(*Effects?*) Having to lie to employers who want to know why I was only in service one year. I tell them I got a Medical Discharge.

After [having trouble with] the federal government I've never mentioned discharge. I've always put down General and nothing has happened.

In the beginning, looking for jobs, employers did ask for discharge papers but weren't too insistent. That was easily avoided by saying I was 4F.

Either saying they had not been in the military, or if they had, saying that they had had a discharge different from the one they received, constitutes an important method of avoiding the consequences of a less than honorable discharge, though it seems less common than applying for jobs where discharges will not be asked for.

As well as "bold-faced lying," we found other methods whereby the character of the discharge was concealed. In three cases which involved enlisted men who had served for some time, the following method was used. After every enlistment period is up, the serviceman is given an Honorable Discharge and immediately signs up for the next period of enlistment. In the cases mentioned above, even though this final enlistment period was terminated with a less than honorable discharge, they used their Honorable Discharges from other periods when they applied for jobs.

I had an Honorable Discharge in 1956. I got the Honorable in March for re-enlistment—you get discharged and re-enlist again, it's a formality. Then I got the Undesirable in September. . . . I show the Honorable one if anyone asks. I've got away with it ten years.

Another case is interesting for its ingenuity.

I've avoided telling [anyone] about my discharge; the guy I work for now said, "I assume you have an Honorable Discharge," and I said, "Yes." The bank asked though [when I went for a loan]. I simply Xeroxed the thing [the discharge] with the words "under other than" removed, and showed it to them. I got my check.

Thus, in most cases, adjustment does not seem too difficult. Either it involves going for jobs where the question of discharge does not come up or lying when it does. Where it is most problematic is where one cannot take advantage of one's training or experience, which usually occurs in jobs that require security clearance. In these cases there is usually a feeling of great hardship and frustration.

Another major effect which we expected as a result of receiving a less than honorable discharge was that the individual's family would come to know that one of their members was homosexual. This was so, not only because of investigating agencies questioning persons in his community, but also because of the questions inevitably raised over failure to complete the requisite time in the military.

Only 8 persons, however, said that their families knew they were homosexual on account of their discharge. Of these, 5 told their families themselves, and 3 came to the attention of their families because of the activities of the military.

What accounts for the remaining 23 being able to hide the fact of their discharge from their families? The simple answer to this is that the majority of them lied. The lie consisted of telling their families that they had had an Honorable or a Medical Discharge for some reason or other, the favored one being for "nervous breakdown." Other cases involved enlisted men who said they got fed up with military life and got out; in many cases deception was not necessary among these people, as their families were not sure of the length of enlistment anyway. Finally there were those who were in some way estranged from their families. This included those whose parents were dead, those who lived away from home, and those who did not return home after their separation from the military. In addition, military investigators usually are bluffing when they say they will investigate in the suspect's home community (we found only one such case) and for our sample, anyway, the majority did serve lengthy periods before they were discharged.

INTERPRETATIONS OF SUBJECTIVE EFFECTS

Though objectively the effects of the discharge upon a person may be slight, subjectively he may have very strong feelings, fears or hesitations about having received such a stigma. From the report of our respondents it was evident that after employment, the most important effect of receiving a less than honorable discharge centered on one or another subjective state.

In the main there were five types of feelings expressed about receiving a less than honorable discharge. The response to the question of how they felt included feelings at the time they received the discharge and how they felt at the time of our interview. At the time of our interview, feelings were more controlled than when the experience actually happened. (No attempt has been made on our part to separate these two time periods in the following analysis.) Types of predominant feelings and their distributions are presented in Table 35.

Table 35. Subjective Responses to Receiving a Less Than Honorable Discharge

PREDOMINANT RESPONSE	(N = 31)
Anger, annoyance, irritation	10%
Guilt, shame, mortification	26
Collapse, confusion, disorientation	12
Sense of injustice	32
No feelings or "couldn't care less"	19

ANGER, ANNOYANCE, IRRITATION

Here the discharge did not seem to play a large part in the person's life. It was defined more as a minor irritant, an annoying thing at the time, but since then of little consequence.

GUILT, SHAME, MORTIFICATION

These cases included people who, at least initially, accepted the view of the military—they had been defined as undesirables and came to take it as a true depiction of themselves. The result was a great feeling of guilt.

I'm always cringing in a group of straight people when the subject of service is brought up and having to lie about it. . . . I feel a little inferior for the fact of not having finished the service.

It's kind of funny to see a guy with thirteen years' service experience told that he's unfit for service. . . . I was really at the lowest point of my life. . . . I was contemplating suicide. . . . I've still got a guilt complex, not as much now, but I used to think that everyone I looked at was saying "there goes that queer." . . . I give it [the whole experience] little thought these days.

The following we saw as more indicative of shame than guilt. It should be of no surprise that there are among homosexuals, as among heterosexuals, persons who wish to perform what they call "their duty" to their country and are upset when this opportunity is denied to them. This is especially the case for those discharged during wartime.

I felt my life and future had been ruined. It made me feel like I had failed my country and I had failed God. It just made me feel like a failure. I contemplated suicide but thank God I had the strength to go on. I was forced into gay life because of this discharge because you know you can't straighten out your life because this is always hanging over your head. . . . I had to have gay friends because straight people always talk about the service and I didn't want to lie so I left them so they wouldn't find out.

At the time I felt terrible I couldn't do more for those guys who got maimed and wounded, and I couldn't fulfill my duty. A few times that has come and hit me hard. All those guys gave up so much and I didn't fullfill my end of it. [R discharged during the Second World War.]

The lame duck that Veterans were wearing, I didn't get one. It showed you were a veteran and had done service. My friends and relations, although they didn't ask me, they might have wondered, particularly as I was discharged in 1944 just before the end of the war.

COLLAPSE, CONFUSION, DISORIENTATION

These respondents were shocked by the whole experience and either found it difficult to adjust to their new status or made adjustments that caused further problems. Two subjects in this category were removed to psychiatric wards because of their reaction. The following quotation from an enlisted man describes the disorientation that can occur in the face of the experience.

I was very depressed and upset. A major part of my adult life had been spent in the Navy. It's like going home and finding someone's murdered your wife and children and burned down your home. Ninety-five per cent of your life is ended right there. All my friends were in the Navy and I was cut off from them.

SENSE OF INJUSTICE

The most common feeling that runs through the accounts given by our respondents is that which we term "sense of injustice."

This response centers on the unfairness of the military toward what the respondent sees as a relatively harmless offense.

I would have been a career man. My personal opinion is that for the offense the discharge is adequate. But I had medals and a good record. I was gung-ho all the way. I feel these things should weigh in the balance. . . . If the military would recognize the fact . . . homosexuals may not make first-line soldiers but there are a hell of a lot of us who have been combat soldiers. I say let them prove themselves.

I felt I didn't deserve the type of discharge I'd gotten and under those circumstances that I'd had to go into the service at all.

I was hurt and felt it was unjustified.

Resentment, because I still don't think I've done anything wrong.

It was grossly damaging to me personally, out of all proportion to what I'd done.

The whole attitude seems to be not wanted around the government at all—they don't want anything to do with me, just collect my taxes and shove me off into the corner. . . . The flaming faggots aren't going to make it in the service, but if they've done their jobs they should be given an Honorable Discharge.

I really don't give a fuck. I'd like to get it changed some day though. (Why?) Just to fuck up the military. It was a shitty way of treating me but now I really couldn't care.

NO FEELINGS OR "COULDN'T CARE LESS"

These are those respondents who say the discharge had little effect—who just wanted to get out of the service and often had turned themselves in.

A final point we think is of interest is what the respondent felt about military service prior to getting into trouble. Of the 30 who answered the question "Would you have liked to remain in the service?," 15 (or 50 percent) say Yes they would have. When we asked both groups how enjoyable service life was for them, we found no significant difference between the groups, a majority in each defining the experience as very enjoyable (Table 36).

Table 36. Enjoyment of Service Life, by Discharge Status

	TYPE OF DISCHARGE	
SERVICE LIFE WAS:	HD (N = 32)	LHD* (N = 31)
Very enjoyable	53%	39%
Somewhat enjoyable	16	29
Not very enjoyable	22	16
Not enjoyable at all	9	16

When frequencies are combined in rows 2–4, $\gamma = .28$, $z = 0.895$, two-tailed $p = .372$.

* For the LHD group, the question referred to the time before they got into trouble.

Chapter 10

THE EFFECTS OF BEING OFFICIALLY LABELED: SUBJECTIVE DIFFERENCES BETWEEN THE GROUPS

In the last chapter, we examined how our respondents interpreted the effect of their less than honorable discharge on their lives. We now look at their life situations at the time of the interview as compared to homosexuals who received an Honorable Discharge.

It will be remembered that comparing the IID and LIID groups on certain variables that referred to their preinduction situation, the LHD group was found to be further advanced in their homosexual careers than the HD group. In our analysis we take account of this difference; as the largest difference in homosexual career was in frequency of homosexual sex prior to induction, this is introduced as a third variable to check for any possible spurious relationships (that is, that differences found cannot be attributed to the effects of discharge but to the difference in the stage of homosexual career prior to induction). In addition, it is theoretically those persons less advanced in their homosexual careers prior to induction that are of most interest. It is in this group that we expect to find most change according to labeling theory. Therefore it is important to be able to isolate this group and examine it in comparison to its control in the partial. If we have been speaking previously of spuriousness, in this case we are talking of specification.

We, therefore, introduced the variable of prior sex frequency where we thought fit. For differences that might have been explained by prior sex frequency, it was introduced to check for spurious findings; in those cases where statistically significant differences appeared or percentage differences were quite large even though not significant, prior sex frequency was introduced in an attempt to specify relationships. Of course, in certain cases, the introduction of this variable was not possible, as the particular distributions on the original relationship did not allow for partialing. In *all* the multivariate runs relevant to this chapter and the next chapter, however, prior sex frequency produced no significant effects; thus these additional runs are not discussed. The test for specification employed was Leo Goodman's method for analyzing three-factor interaction in contingency tables.

SUBJECTIVE DIFFERENCES BETWEEN THE GROUPS

The following data were gathered primarily by means of the open-ended interview in an attempt to get at the respondent's subjective feelings about himself and his way of life. The various hypotheses to be tested using data from this source are outlined in Chapter 1.

SELF-ACCEPTANCE

We have said that as a deviant status, being homosexual often becomes the individual's master status. This occurs only after an individual's deviance becomes known to others who then reconstitute his social identity. Such a master status is stigmatic, and the self-judgments of the officially labeled may become reflections of these social judgments. This is another way of saying that those deviants who have had their deviance officially examined are likely to be less accepting of themselves than those to whom this experience has not occurred. This does not mean we are ignoring the possible psychic costs of secret deviance which also revolve around the acceptance of a deviant self, only that official degradation makes self-acceptance more difficult. A number of indicants were used to get at self-acceptance. The first was a question on the close-ended questionnaire which asked respondents to agree or disagree with the statement, "I wish I could have more respect for myself." Results are shown in Table 37.

Table 37. Respect for Self, by Discharge Status

I WISH I COULD HAVE MORE RESPECT FOR MYSELF	DISCHARGE STATUS	
	HD (N = 32)	LHD (N = 30)
Strongly agree	6%	10%
Agree	25	10
Disagree	47	47
Strongly disagree	22	33

When frequencies are combined in rows 1–2 and 3–4, $\gamma = .29$, $z = 0.715$, two-tailed $p = .474$.

Sixty-nine percent (22) of the HD group did not agree with the statement compared to 80 percent (24) of the LHD group; this difference is not only nonsignificant but in the opposite direction to what was predicted. All other questions asked were open-ended questions from the interview.

Respondents were first asked, "In general, what do you think of yourself?" The replies to this question were coded along the various parameters of self described by Chad Gordon.[1] No striking differences were found, as can be seen in Table 38 (except in the item coded "Sense of self-determination," where the difference between the groups was largest; although one of Gordon's dimensions, it was of no theoretical importance to us as operationalized by him).

To get at self-acceptance, the number of positive descriptions as against negative were counted, and the respondent was coded as having a predominantly positive or negative picture of himself. The results of this procedure appear in Table 39. No significant differences appear using this method, both groups distributing similarly in their evaluations of self. As an illustration of what we called a predominantly positive evaluation we offer the following self-description.

[1] Chad Gordon, "Self Conceptions: Configurations of Content," in Chad Gordon and Kenneth J. Gergen (eds.), *The Self in Social Interaction* (New York: Wiley, 1968), pp. 115–36.

Table 38. Self-Description, by Discharge Status

	DISCHARGE STATUS	
PREDOMINANTLY DESCRIBES SELF IN TERMS OF:	HD (N = 32)	LHD (N = 29)
Sense of moral worth (good, bad, reliable, responsible, loyal, etc.)	28%	24%
Sense of self-determination (ambitious, adventurous, trying to get ahead)	3	24
Sense of unity (mixed up, ambivalent, straightened out now, adjusted)	13	17
Sense of competence (intelligent, creative, not using potential)	28	21
Abstract identification (individual, unique, indefinable, average)	13	3
Interpersonal style (quiet, shy, affectionate, how usually acts)	13	3
Psychic style (how usually thinks, feels: happy, sad, curious)	3	7
Interests and activities (judgments, taste)	0	0
External meanings (judgments of others; well-liked, respected)	0	0

When frequencies are combined in rows 1 and 3–9, $\gamma = -.82$, $z = 2.031$, two-tailed $p = .042$.

Table 39. Self-Evaluation, by Discharge Status

	DISCHARGE STATUS	
SELF-DESCRIPTION	HD (N = 32)	LHD (N = 29)
Predominantly positive	63%	66%
Predominantly neutral	16	13
Predominantly negative	22	21

When frequencies are combined in rows 2–3 $\gamma = -.05$, $z = 0.091$, two-tailed $p = .928$.

On the good side, I'm friendly and try to get along with people—I'm sentimental, generous. On the other hand I'm stubborn. I'm friendly to a certain point, perhaps that's why I live alone. I don't get drunk or throw away money. I try to live halfway decently, but I'm no angel. I don't dislike the kind of person I am. I don't think I would try and change myself too much.

Next is a case illustrative of a predominantly negative evaluation.

I have a very poor opinion of myself because I don't think I'm using my full potential intellect. Socially I'm not the toast of the town; sexually I'm nothing to boast about—people don't faint with desire when I walk down the street. . . . I'm not very aggressive and resourceful: meeting new situations I'm in agony. I'm not sure of myself and I withdraw.

Finally, we asked the respondent directly, "Do you like the kind of person you are?" The results are shown in Table 40.

Table 40. Self-Acceptance, by Discharge Status

| SELF-ACCEPTANCE | DISCHARGE STATUS | |
	HD (N = 32)	LHD (N = 29)
Likes the person he is	78%	76%
Does not like the person he is	22	24

$\gamma = .09$, $z = -0.094$, one-tailed $p = .462$.

Again there are no significant differences between the two groups in the replies to the question.

A comparable question asked of Chicago respondents was to what extent they agreed that there are many things about themselves they would like to change. Forty-six percent (22) of the HD group thought there was (at least sometimes) compared to 74 percent (23) of the LHD group. This is a significant difference in the direction originally predicted ($\gamma = .55$, $z = 2.470$, one-tailed $p = .007$).

It was thought that aspects of self *other* than sexual orientation might mask how one felt about his deviance. Consequently a question was taken from the Institute for Sex Research's Chicago questionnaire which we thought best reflected the respondent's acceptance of the "deviant" aspect of his self. The question asked was, "If there were a magic pill that would make you completely and permanently heterosexual, would you take such a pill today?" The results from this question are shown in Table 41. No

Table 41. Acceptance of Homosexuality, by Discharge Status

	DISCHARGE STATUS	
WOULD TAKE PILL	HD (N = 32)	LHD (N = 30)
Yes	19%	13%
No	81	87

$\gamma = .20$, $z = 0.232$, two-tailed $p = .816$.

significant differences appear between our groups, the majority in each apparently accepting their homosexuality.

The corresponding data from the Chicago study are similar. Seventy-four percent (34) of the HD group and 78 percent (25) of the LHD group would not take such a pill. Again there are no significant differences between HD and LHD groups ($\gamma = -.11$, $z = -0.423$, two-tailed $p = .672$).

In addition the Chicago respondents were asked if they had ever seriously considered discontinuing their homosexuality. Sixty-three percent (30) of the HD group and 56 percent (18) of the LHD group said No ($\gamma = .13$, $z = 0.555$, one-tailed $p = .291$). Also the question was raised if they regretted being homosexual in any way. Forty-six percent (22) of the HD group said No compared to 41 percent (13) of the LHD group, again a nonsignificant difference ($\gamma = .10$, $z = 0.457$, one-tailed $p = .444$).

We also asked why such a decision would be made. Because most people answered No, we shall only be concerned with the reasons given for such negative decisions. How respondents were distributed with regard to such reasons is presented in Table 42.

The majority of replies from both groups centered on the desire to maintain the status quo. Although many respondents had had problems in the past regarding their homosexuality, most now seemed to have arrived at a satisfactory adjustment to being homosexual and were loath to depart from this state of affairs into something they were not sure of. Answers illustrative of this category follow below.

Forget it! (*Are you happy as you are?*) Very much so—it took me too long a time to go through learning about it [homosexuality] to change. I'm just happy where I am.

Table 42. Reasons Given for *Not* Taking the "Magic Pill," by Discharge Status

REASONS GIVEN FOR *Not* TAKING THE PILL	DISCHARGE STATUS	
	HD (N = 26)	LHD (N = 23)*
Satisfied with self: happy as I am: no advantage	37%	48%
Not "normal": sexuality is part of me	15	22
Fear of the unknown: risk of unhappiness	8	9
Feel out of place: no guidelines	4	0
Would dislike women	8	4
Would require a "total" change of life	15	17
Wouldn't give up partner	12	0

* Three persons did not provide answers that were codable. The largest difference occurs in row 7. Combining frequencies in all other rows, $\gamma = 1.000$, $z = 1.073$, two-tailed $p = .290$.

I basically have no desire to be heterosexual. I don't want a close relationship with a woman; I don't want children. I have heterosexual girl friends I adore, but I'd just as soon go to bed with my dog. I prefer men.

No, I don't see why heterosexuality is so great. I'd be the same person, I'd have the same problems. I'd just have a different sexual orientation. (*Would your life be easier?*) No, I don't think so.

The next most common response involved the evaluation of sexuality as an integral part of the personality, a part that greatly determined a lot of other things, so that if sexual orientation were changed then it would be impossible to be the "same person."

No, the pill would also have to change every aspect of my being—my attitude toward women as persons, birth control, economic attitudes and goals, attitudes toward children. You'd have another person. If I changed now I'd kill my wife. (*What wife?*) The one I got as a result of the pill.

No, I wouldn't, and that goes for anything that would change me. I'd rather be myself and if I have my problems I'll cope with them.

No . . . it's a complete transition of the person; it would take a complete reorientation of an individual . . . to blot out everything and teach him individuality again.

The next most frequent answer referred to a complete change in the way of life that they now led (rather than to a complete change of personality). Respondents were reluctant to give up this way of life totally, which they felt taking the pill would entail.

At age ten I'm sure I would, but now I wouldn't want to take half of my life and say that it's been no use to me. To say the patterns I've developed, the friendships, the relationships were no good, I couldn't do it. I wouldn't want to.

I'd be very much out of place suddenly. My friends for the most part are gay, my trade is a gay trade and so things would be different. (*Would you be happier?*) Being straight is no sure way to happiness.

The other reasons given were less common than the three types illustrated above. Because of this we feel that it is not important to examine them at this time. Reasons for taking or not taking the pill were not asked in the Chicago study.

SELF AS DETERMINED

The next aspect of self considered was whether or not the respondent felt he was responsible for being homosexual, whether it had been a process over which he had had much control. It has been shown in studies of other deviants that seeing oneself as "acted upon rather than acting" is a common excuse among those who are confronted with their deviance and asked to give an account of themselves by the conventional world.[2] We thus expected more of our LHD group to report that the deviant part of their selves was something over which they had no control. First, we asked if they thought that it was inevitable that they became homosexual, with the results as follows: 66 percent (21) of the HD group thought it was inevitable compared to 80 percent (24) of the LHD group. This difference is not large enough to be significant ($\gamma = -.28$, $z = 0.750$, one-tailed $p = .226$). Illustrative of the remarks we took as reflecting inevitability are the following:

---

[2] Gresham M. Sykes and David Matza, "Techniques of Neutralization: A Theory of Delinquency," *American Sociological Review*, 22 (December 1957), 664–70.

It's a culmination of a long train of things [his homosexuality]. If you use certain ingredients in a chemical formula you are going to end up with a certain result. I had the ingredients that made it inevitable. Things were heavily weighted in favor of homosexuality.

Yes it was inevitable, considering the type of life, the things I've read and the people I've had as friends. Even before I had [homosexual] experiences I made friends with people who were homosexual. . . . As I look back on it it couldn't have come out any different.

A second question asked if, in general, they thought it was possible to change homosexuals to exclusive heterosexuality. Seventy-four percent (23) of the HD group said Yes to this, compared to only 50 percent (15) of the LHD group. This difference is large enough to be significant ($\gamma = .46$, $z = 1.727$, one-tailed $p = .042$).

The Chicago study also had a question which reflects the element of choice in becoming homosexual. Respondents were asked the extent to which they agreed with the statement, "Homosexuality is inborn: that is, people are born homosexual or heterosexual." Fifteen percent (7) of the HD group thought this to be true compared to 12 percent (4) of the LHD group. This difference is not significant ($\gamma = -.10$, $z = -0.299$, two-tailed $p = .764$).

Also in the Chicago study, respondents' agreement with the following statement was sought: "People who are homosexual can be changed to heterosexual if only they want to be." Sixty-three percent (30) of the HD group agreed with this compared to 50 percent (16) of the LHD group. Again, this difference is not significant ($\gamma = -.25$, $z = -1.101$, one-tailed $p = .131$).

SELF AS NORMAL

The homosexual often denies the auxiliary traits contained in the stereotype of the homosexual and the degree to which homosexuals and heterosexuals are different (in any way other than their sexual behavior). The homosexual less than honorably discharged, having been treated as an "undesirable," may internalize various aspects of this degradation and be more likely to feel he is different or "abnormal" (dissonance theorists might, however, hypothesize the opposite).

We asked a set of questions on the respondent's perception of the differences between homosexuals and heterosexuals, with the expectation that the HD group would report less difference than would the LHD group.

We first asked them to compare themselves to heterosexuals they knew and tell us the extent to which they differed from them. Seventy-five percent (24) of the HD group stated that they felt there was no difference or little difference (apart from sexual orientation) between themselves and most heterosexuals they knew compared to 70 percent (21) of the LHD group; this difference being nonsignificant ($\gamma = .18$, $z = 0.355$, one-tailed $p = .360$). This question was also asked in the Chicago study with the following results: 68 percent (32) of the HD group saw no difference (or only differences in sexual preference) between homosexuals and heterosexuals compared to 47 percent (15) of the LHD group. This difference is significant ($\gamma = .38$, $z = -1.750$, one-tailed $p = .040$). We also asked in our study whether they believed that most people have both homosexual and heterosexual orientations. Seventy-five percent (24) of the HD group agreed that this was the case compared with 87 percent (26) of the LHD group; this difference is not significant ($\gamma = -.27$, $z = 0.554$, two-tailed $p = .578$).

Most of the reasons offered for this belief centered either on quasi-biological or psychological theories of sexuality or came from their own experience with "straight" males. Some of the more abstract reasons showed evidence of the respondents' having read academic materials on homosexuality.

Definitely, just observe children—till they grow up they are both masculine and feminine till the boy is taught not to cry and the girl told to play with dolls. . . . The child emulates one person or the other. I think I'm typical—I had a dominant mother and a weak father and tended to copy my mother. That's very typical isn't it?

These ranged from fairly precise summaries of intellectual theories to garbled versions of the same interspersed with their own theorizing. More common, however, were reasons that were based on their own interaction with persons they called hetero-sexuals.

[In] certain relationships with male friends of mine, there's a sexual undercurrent which will never be expressed. There's a lot of physical contact between us—not sexual—in some cases if I made some overt move it might develop into something. (*Example?*) Things like—a friend whose wife is away and who will call and have dinner and as we're leaving will put an arm around me or the handshake will be a little too long and strong which on other occasions would be my cue to move in.

. . . straight men who have been interested in me, not sexually, have expressed their interest in a very suspicious way. One of our supervisors calls me "honey baby." I feel such jokes don't come from nowhere. . . . No straight man is interested in me unless he has that vague longing. . . .

I've just accepted it as a fact. I have no proof of it but there is no doubt in my mind it's true. I've observed men in general, in a restroom, looking to see what the fellow next to him has.

Common among these explanations were those occasions where sex took place between the respondent and the purported heterosexual.

Yes, I've slept with as many married guys as single and for the most part they're safer. . . . [Also] I had an experience in Detroit. I met a guy and took him up to my room and he said, "Do whatever you want," so I performed anal intercourse on him and he said, "Thanks, I always wanted to know what you guys did," and he left.

My studies in psychology lead me to believe that everyone has instincts on both sides [homosexual and heterosexual] and I've been to bed with straight people.

There were no large differences found between our groups in the type of reasons given for holding the belief that most people had both homosexual and heterosexual orientations.

Next we asked them of the heterosexuals they had met, what proportion did they think were psychologically disturbed; also what proportion of the homosexuals they had met. This allowed us to compute whether they saw similarities or differences in psychological disturbance according to sexual orientation. The results are shown in Table 43. Similar proportions in both groups saw no

Table 43. **Perceptions of Psychological Disturbance, by Discharge Status**

EXTENT OF PSYCHOLOGICAL DISTURBANCES	DISCHARGE STATUS	
	HD (N = 32)	LHD (N = 30)
Heterosexuals more than homosexuals	0%	10%
Homosexuals more than heterosexuals	34	27
About the same	59	53
Don't know	6	10

When frequencies are combined in rows 1 and 2 and row 4 excluded, $\gamma = -.08$, $z = 0.042$, two-tailed $p = .966$.

difference between homosexuals and heterosexuals, and this was the modal response.

An associated question we asked here also was if they thought themselves to be psychologically disturbed in any way. Forty-five percent (14) of the HD group said Yes to this question compared to 31 percent (9) of the LHD group. This difference is not significant, however ($\gamma = .31$, $z = 0.943$, two-tailed $p = .344$).

We found no differences either in the reasons given by respondents as to why they thought they were psychologically disturbed. These seemed to fall into two general categories: difficulties in adjusting socially to being a homosexual; and "psychological" problems, sometimes growing out of the problems of social adjustment and sometimes not. This latter category included, for example, problems arising from not being able to accept homosexuality as part of oneself. Using these two broad categories, of those saying that they were psychologically disturbed, 64 percent (9) of the HD group gave "psychological reasons" compared to 56 percent (5) of the LHD group. The corresponding figures for "social" reasons were 36 percent (5) and 44 percent (4), respectively. These differences are not significant (Fisher's Exact Test).

Some explanations involving social pressures were quite direct.

The evidence points strongly in that direction, I've been in psychiatric wards twice. (*Why?*) Because of the lack of approbation that society has for any form of sexuality.

All homosexuals have some disturbance about doing something taboo to society. . . . This has given them guilt feelings, anxieties and it's really bad. . . . I worry about what people think. In my business, if people found out it would ruin me.

Other reasons involved interpersonal problems, especially with other homosexuals.

[Because of] jealousy. I guess this is because of insecurities. I suffered very much from this when I was in a deeply involved homosexual relationship some years ago, and I still suffer.

I have problems relating to people. I have trouble with the intensity of the relationship; I have many, many casual friends. It's a common thing with homosexuals. It has to do with the question of spontaneity, concealing one's feelings. It's difficult to find a balance between discretion and spontaneity.

[Because] there's a certain loneliness to the life, a certain impermanence, a lack of any deep meaning with partners. . . .

Those reasons we defined as psychological included problems over accepting homosexuality, and although they involved social pressures they differed from the above in that the person had *yet* to accept himself as homosexual.

I still have some guilt that I can't work through, I still have some self doubt.

It's possible that homosexuality isn't necessarily of itself a problem —like bad eyesight if we could get spectacles. But I would prefer 20/20 vision with spectacles.

Most answers, however, involved some use of psychological terminology in a commonsense way.

Yes, I tend to be a little paranoiac. I'm hypersensitive to people's reactions to me. I tend to magnify someone's thoughtlessness as a rebuff.

Yes, but I'm gradually coming out of the obsessions I have. . . .
My normal adjustment was stopped; I went to a private school and
had homosexual sex there. My father found out and tried to stop it.
I stopped myself which was the worst thing that ever happened. I
got obsessed with the idea of homosexuality without doing anything
about it. I repressed myself badly.

I'm more or less a schizoid personality. I don't relate to people the
way one is supposed to. I don't develop normal interpersonal relationships, but what is normal? I don't know.

SELF AS A PRACTICAL METHODOLOGIST

We said that one of the secondary gains of being deviant is an
uncommon knowledge of social structures. Just as many sociologists who study deviance claim that this is an excellent way to
study conformity, the officially labeled deviant, through his practical study of society's reaction to him, gains "insight" into the
process of how morality is socially produced and sustained. He
has been a central figure in a degradation ceremony and experienced the force of moral condemnation. As against those deviants
who have not been officially labeled, we would expect him, therefore, to claim more knowledge of how the world works. We
asked our respondents, "Do you think that being homosexual has
made you more knowledgeable about life in general?" The results
are shown in Table 44. As can be seen, we do get a large differ-

Table 44. Knowledge of Life in General, by Discharge Status

MORE KNOWLEDGEABLE ABOUT LIFE IN GENERAL	DISCHARGE STATUS	
	HD (N = 32)	LHD (N = 30)
Yes	66%	87%
No	34	13

$\gamma = -.55$, $z = 1.623$, one-tailed $p = .052$.

ence in the predicted direction, significant at the .052 level (one-
tailed). No comparable item was asked of Chicago respondents.

The reasons given by respondents for such knowledge are
provided in Table 45. The modal response from those who an-

Table 45. Reasons for Increased Knowledge of Life, by Discharge Status

REASONS FOR INCREASED KNOWLEDGE	DISCHARGE STATUS	
	HD (N = 20)*	LHD (N = 24)
Necessary for self-defense; adjustment	5%	25%
Increased social horizons; not restricted to traditional life	45	38
Through own suffering: more sensitive	40	29
Forced personal reflection	10	6

* One respondent from the HD group and two from the LHD group did not provide a reason.
When frequencies are combined in rows 2–4, the difference between discharge status and reasons for increased knowledge provides a two-tailed Fisher's Exact $p = .158$.

swered positively among both groups referred to the social life that was possible for homosexuals who, free of family and other restrictions, could meet a variety of people for sexual or social reasons. As such, it "broadens their horizons."

It gives me a broader outlook on life. If you're heterosexual you have to think of the family first before you make any move. . . . I'm more independent. I'm free, I have no ties whatsoever. I don't have anything to tie me down like a family so my mind's free to think of other things.

If I was a heterosexual with kids I'd have them around me all the time. You give up your life for children—therefore give up your breadth of knowledge. I see this with a wife too. A guy goes to work and gives his paycheck to that cunt, he gets home and she sticks the kids on him. I think heterosexuals are nuts. Knowledge comes from travel and things like that and if you're not tied down in a family you can experience more things.

A person who gets married at a younger age goes into a cocoon. His family is his entire life. I've had more freedom. I could travel. I've had more social contacts, more jobs, a much wider experience.

The next most frequent reason offered, again with little difference between the groups, was that being homosexual entailed a good deal of suffering, and this suffering made homosexuals more sensitive to other people and their problems, thus more empathetic and understanding of people in general. The comparison was often made between homosexuals as a minority group and other minority groups like blacks. Respondents claimed being more knowledgeable about the black revolt because they understood what it was like to be a minority.

Being a member of a minority group makes you more knowledgeable or aware of life going on around you. (*Why?*) I just think one is.

Yes, first we are aware of people's feelings more so than most heterosexuals. (*Why?*) Because we are sensitive about our own feelings. We don't like to be constantly the butt end of jokes or constantly called sick. Because we are sensitive about our feelings we are more sensitive about others. Often we are overly so because we can understand better.

. . . having known closely a number of people who have lived under the difficult conditions that most homosexuals live under has made me more sensitive to other people.

Yes, definitely. You accept people for what they are, you're less prejudiced, you're not drawn to one particular type of person. . . . You just live and let live more.

Another theme we coded as "Forced Personal Reflection," the nature of which is apparent from the following quotations:

Yes, very much so, especially in my category . . . you must remember you're Negro and homosexual so that's two strikes against you. You must bring your level of intelligence up to beat the strikes, so I think I'm better versed in most subjects than the normal heterosexual.

The headman [psychiatrist] talked turkey. He said, "You're intelligent; if you're going this route be careful and don't create a problem for yourself and other people." That's what I mean by more insight.

In one category, we did find a sizable difference (though nonsignificant) between our groups. This centered on the following reason: that gaining knowledge of the way society operated was essential because it was an efficient way to protect oneself from the social punishments that accrue from being deviant. Five percent (1) of the HD group gave this as a reason

as compared to 25 percent (6) of the LHD group. The following
are illustrations of this "reason":

It's given me a certain fox-and-hounds shrewdness and has forced
me to look at many things I couldn't have seen otherwise because I
wouldn't have needed to see them. (*What like?*) The ability to take
social disguises, alertness for danger in social situations, the fact that
detection of my homosexuality would have meant problems. . . .
You become more alert and more aware because it's necessary, it's
like the fox being able to hear the hounds baying even though they're
not in earshot . . . it's sort of a supersensitiveness, to danger . . .
[it's] self-preservation.

Having to lead a secret life sharpens your sensibilities to what
other people are thinking or liable to do.

I'm better able to normalize myself in society. (*What do you mean?*)
Have a situation where I can revolve in society without being nervous
or having any trouble. I've learned to put up a show to fool the
straight world.

When a person's put on the defensive all the time he's more alert
to life. He gets more out of life, he sees more, he's on the ball.

Whether or not homosexuals or any other deviants do "know
more" about society in general is questionable, but it is apparent
that many feel they do. Few answered as candidly as the following respondent, who pinpointed the problem in making such
claims.

I firmly believe in Goethe's dictum, "Nobody knows his own
language until he knows another." This puts me in an embarrassing
position, though, as I really don't know much about heterosexuals.

SENSE OF EXPOSURE

Having a secret differentness, there is always the possibility of
exposure. This often leads to a sense of vulnerability. The person
feels he stands out in a crowd and that "everybody knows" that
he is presenting an inauthentic self. We claim that this is characteristic of most deviants and that this is a tribute to the power of
conventional moral forces. It is difficult to accept one's deviance
completely, and even if successful, exposure to nondeviants can

be an undesired event. This sense of exposure is felt more, we predicted, by the officially labeled deviant whose deviance is a matter of record and who has been exposed, pulled from a group and made to stand alone and confront his differentness.

To get at feelings of exposure and vulnerability, we asked respondents, "In day-to-day situations do you think that it is easy for people to tell that you are a homosexual?" The majority of persons in both groups, 88 percent (28) in the HD group and 90 percent (27) in the LHD group, said that they did not think this was so ($\gamma = .02$, $z = -0.327$, two-tailed $p = .744$). We also asked, "Can other homosexuals tell (that you are homosexual) without you doing anything special?" Forty-four percent (14) of the HD group said Yes compared to 60 percent (18) of the LHD group, this difference being nonsignificant ($\gamma = -.28$, $z = 0.877$, one-tailed $p = .483$).

It is of further interest to note that those who claimed that other homosexuals could tell, all gave more or less the same reason why. This involved various versions of the folk saying, "It takes one to know one." How "one knew one," however, was not so easily established. No respondent gave a really clear answer when questioned on this, the clearest involving the matter of locale; if a person was seen on a certain street or in a certain bar, it was inferred that he was homosexual. Other than this, a common answer was "eye contact," "the way he looks at you."

Just a look, you look at a heterosexual man and if you catch his eye he'll go straight on, whereas a gay person will look a moment. The clothing, where you're at, it's another sense you pick up. (*Tell me more about the look.*) Oh! their eyes scan you and your body.

"It takes one to know one" because we do recognize each other. . . . It's a keenly developed sense, for one thing, homosexuals want to spot others . . . you develop a sixth sense.

Yes, as they say, "It takes one to know one." (*How?*) We've got a sixth sense. (*What do you mean?*) I don't know, maybe the way you look at them.

I'd say Yes, from the way they look at me. I feel I think they know, maybe they don't. Location could pinpoint me; appearance, voice, could give me away. Maybe I'm obvious, who knows?

I would say Yes. (How?) I feel there's a great deal of nonverbal communication between people. The hippies call it "vibrations." Sometimes it's just the way people look. (How?) Maybe a little longer than usual.

The second set of questions on the interview moved from self-perceptions and typifications to the perception and typification of other people. That is, what our respondents reported other people to think and feel about homosexuals.

RECIPROCITY OF PERSPECTIVES

How far do heterosexuals understand what it is like to be a homosexual in this society? How deep does sympathy or under-standing go? We wanted to see how much homosexuals felt they were cut off from heterosexuals by virtue of their deviance; to what extent was there a lack of intersubjectivity. We began by asking our respondents what they thought most "straight people" think of homosexuals. Most of the answers showed that our re-spondents felt that heterosexuals held negative stereotypes of homosexuals. We had predicted that the LHD group would hold the most negative view of what heterosexuals thought of them, but no significant differences appeared. The results can be seen in Table 46.

Table 46. Perception of Heterosexuals' View of Homosexuals, by Discharge Status

HETEROSEXUALS VIEW HOMOSEXUALS AS:	DISCHARGE STATUS	
	HD (N = 32)	LHD (N = 30)
Psychologically sick	3%	13%
Immoral	0	0
Dangerous	13	23
Effeminate, swishy, amusing	28	17
Mainly like other people	0	3
Tolerant or ignored them	16	30
Qualified answer	34	10
Don't know	6	3

When row 8 is excluded and when frequencies are combined in rows 1–4 and 5–7, $\gamma = -.17$, $z = 0.389$, one-tailed $p = .448$

Qualified answers said that only some heterosexuals hold negative stereotypes, or that perceptions were determined by education and the like. If qualified answers are considered as "not negative," then 44 percent (14) of the HD as compared to 53 percent (16) of the LHD group saw heterosexuals as holding negative stereotypes of them, this difference being statistically nonsignificant ($\gamma = -.17$, $z = 0.389$, one-tailed $p = .448$).

The following are examples of "qualified answers":

I don't know what they think. There's a whole spectrum—from those not giving a shit to those who think homosexuals are the bottom of the barrel.

It runs the whole gamut. It depends on their educational and cultural background and stability in their heterosexuality.

Examples of perceptions of tolerance are:

My impression today is that in this area the attitude is indifferent.

My theory is that they don't think much about them [homosexuals].

I don't think they care one way or the other. . . . I don't think straight people think much about it, frankly.

The other most frequent reply was that the picture most heterosexuals have of homosexuals is the stereotype of the effeminate, swishy, "faggot," exemplified in the following responses:

Most of the straight people I know are heavily influenced by stereotyped judgments, not particularly articulate or verbal. They see homosexuals as pansies or faggots.

That of the classical fairy. The film *The Detective* pointed out the public's view and the police—effeminate gestures, high-pitched voice, and preoccupation with sex.

We next asked a more direct question on reciprocal perspectives which asked, "To what extent do you think that 'straight people' realize what it's like to be a homosexual in this society?" Seventy-eight percent (25) of the HD group said they had no idea at all compared to 60 percent (18) of the LHD group. This difference is opposite to what was predicted and is not significant ($\gamma = -.44$, $z = 1.427$, two-tailed $p = .152$).

Even those who said heterosexuals had "some idea" said this was not really very much of an idea. Thus we coded the answers to the question of what it is they *particularly* misunderstood, using all cases. The results obtained appear in Table 47. Few

Table 47. **Misunderstanding of Homosexuals by Heterosexuals, by Discharge Status**

TYPE OF MISUNDERSTANDING BY HETEROSEXUALS	DISCHARGE STATUS	
	HD (N = 31)	LHD (N = 30)
The nature of homosexual sex and love	35%	27%
The social range of homosexuals	3	0
Believe the stereotype of homosexuals	12	13
Homosexuality is a moral failing	3	7
Homosexuals are psychologically ill	6	20
Generally misunderstood	39	33

The largest difference occurs in row 5. When frequencies are combined in all other rows, $\gamma = -.567$, $z = 1.178$, two-tailed $p = .238$.

differences appeared between our groups in what they thought heterosexuals especially misunderstood about homosexuals. The most frequent reply was that they just generally misunderstood.

I think it's like me and nuclear physics—what is this? I have a feeling they don't understand, and since you've asked why I'm homosexual and I've said I don't know, how are they to know?

There's no particular thing; they get the whole subject in reverse.

It's completely foreign to them. Most heterosexuals have no contact with the homosexual world . . . they don't even recognize homosexuals as existing. You can't realize much if you don't realize it exists.

Of the more specific misunderstandings mentioned, the most common for both groups was that the heterosexual misunderstood the nature of homosexual sex and love.

The primary motivation—that a man likes a man. It's surprising how many women can't understand this. They just don't understand it, period.

They think it's strictly a quick cheap way to have sex.

The personal intimate part of homosexual life, like homosexual marriage—how it can exist, that two homosexuals can live an ordinary life, not one of continual orgies; how two men can lead a married life like a man and a woman.

I don't think it's possible; if you haven't experienced the overt physical thing you can't on an intellectual basis. I think, unfortunately, without specific knowledge of sexual acts, they think it is some sort of sordid business on a degenerate level that is beyond their comprehension.

Again with little difference between the groups, the following reasons appeared in decreasing frequency: first, that most heterosexuals could not understand homosexuals because they were blinded by one or another stereotypical view.

They think that they're child molesters, that they're out after your kids. They say you can't trust them, they're not good risks.

I don't know, I think many heterosexuals think of the homosexual as a monster, an aberration, totally unacceptable.

Next was the statement that the heterosexual just did not understand the problems associated with the social reactions faced by one who is sexually deviant and in a minority.

What it means to be the victim of heterosexual prejudice; they haven't experienced it so they don't understand it.

. . . the difficulties, the unpleasantries, the difficulties with jobs and with the police, the hostilities of heterosexuals.

I don't believe people in a social majority realize what it's like to be a social minority. My problems looking for jobs with my albatross around my neck have given me more insight into the problems blacks have than my parents for instance. (*What albatross?*) My discharge [Undesirable].

Finally, two other reasons were proposed: one, that homosexuality is believed to be a moral failing; and two, that it is some form of psychological or mental illness.

The fact that it is wrong in their [heterosexuals'] eyes.

I guess they think it's a character defect or a moral sin.

. . . they feel it's so morally wrong that we are worthless.

An illustration of a view of "mental illness" is the following:

They feel there must be some psychological maladjustment along the line and they can't accept the idea that one can be homosexual and as fully adjusted to life as any heterosexual could be.

SENSE OF INJUSTICE

We predicted that the officially labeled deviant is more likely to feel a sense of injustice about the way he was treated than the deviant whose deviance remains unknown, and this for a variety of reasons. Most important among these reasons for the homosexual separated less than honorably from the military is the belief that the punishment—to have been stigmatized and prevented from serving out his time and made to face employment difficulties—does not fit the crime and is unjustly disproportionate to his "offense." We already have seen the feelings of injustice among the LHD group. We shall now examine if such feelings become generalized and if they are more characteristic of the LHD group than the HD group.

We asked a general question to get at feelings of injustice: "To what extent do you think that homosexuals are themselves to blame for the reaction society takes toward them?" Only 23 percent (7) of the HD group and 17 percent (5) of the LHD group said homosexuals were *not* to blame at all, this difference being nonsignificant ($\gamma = .18$, $z = 0.257$, two-tailed $p = .760$). The vast majority said homosexuals were to blame, but in *one* respect only. Seventy-four percent (23) of the HD group (96 percent of those saying, Yes) and 70 percent (21) of the LHD group (84 percent of those saying, Yes) said that the negative reaction toward homosexuals came in large part from that minority among homosexuals, the "queens," the effeminate, "swishy" type of individual who flaunts his homosexuality in public. Other than this, only two respondents said homosexuals were to blame at all.

The following quotations are examples of what was said about the "queens":

The lowest elements, the ones who get into a cliché of what a homosexual is—bejeweled, flamboyant types who are doing something very overt and feminine is the stereotype of the homosexual as the drunken Negro bum is an embarrassment to Negroes. Prejudice against a minority is aimed at the obvious bad forms of that minority.

Some homosexuals seem to seek out opportunities which will expose them and some desire to thumb their nose at society and tend to act very obnoxiously in public. Some enjoy sex more if it's in a public park. And because these are the homosexuals to whom people's attention is called, they get their ideas from them.

Finally we asked how, in general, did they react to "straight" people. If they felt unjustly treated by the heterosexual world, then we would expect them to have negative feelings about heterosexuals and avoid them. We thought this would especially characterize the LHD group. No such finding appeared, however; the majority of both groups, 78 percent (25) of the HD and 83 percent (25) of the LHD group, saying that in general their reaction toward "straight people" was positive. This difference is nonsignificant ($\gamma = -.09$, $z = -0.063$, two-tailed $p = .948$).

In conclusion, therefore, few differences were found between our groups as regards their subjective interpretations of themselves and others. No significant differences were found between our groups, with the exception of the following: The LHD group was more likely to deny that homosexuals could be changed to exclusive heterosexuals, and also more likely to believe that being homosexual made them more knowledgeable of life in general.[3]

---

[3] The finding for one of Gordon's categories of self-description is not included because, as noted in the text, it was not a dimension of theoretical interest.

There were few instances where the Chicago data were directly or indirectly comparable. Where this was the case, the results corroborated ours, showing little difference between the HD and LHD groups. Of the differences considered significant in our sample, the first (the belief that it is possible to change homosexuals to heterosexuals) was not supported by a comparable item from the Chicago study. There was no item from the Chicago study with which to compare our second finding (knowledge of life in general). Also, differences considered significant in the Chicago sample were not supported by our data. The Chicago LHD group saw more differences between heterosexuals and homosexuals than did the HD group, and also were more likely to see more things about themselves that they wished to change.

Chapter 11

THE EFFECTS OF BEING OFFICIALLY LABELED: OBJECTIVE DIFFERENCES BETWEEN THE GROUPS

We next consider what we have called the "objective" effects of being labeled deviant. By this we refer to the respondent's activities or behaviors more so than his subjective feelings and interpretations. It will be noted, however, that we do link certain interpretations and actions in this chapter. The data to be reported come from Questionnaire 2 (see Appendix 4).

In Chapter 1 we proposed hypotheses concerning the objective effects of receiving a less than honorable discharge. These discrete hypotheses can be best subsumed under broader headings so that they make more "theoretical sense" when data are brought to bear on them. The first heading refers to the individual's relationship to the homosexual world.

RELATING TO THE HOMOSEXUAL WORLD

One extreme result of being officially labeled deviant is that one's deviance becomes "systematic." Whereas deviant behavior may have been merely an attribute, it now may come to play a larger part in the person's life. It is at this point that we talk less of deviant behavior and more of deviant roles, as a major portion of the person's life becomes organized around managing his deviance.

If this is the case, then we would expect that involvement with other deviants is increased, which further can have the result that the particular form of deviance is easier to carry on as problems of supply and protection are mitigated. Thus, insofar as one of our groups consists of officially labeled homosexuals, we would expect that this group would be more frequent, overt, and exclu-

sive in its deviance and more involved in the homosexual world
and way of life. We examine how far this is supported by the
data.

FREQUENCY OF HOMOSEXUAL SEX

Respondents were asked how often they engaged in homosexual sex at the present time. Table 48 shows there is little

**Table 48. Frequency of Homosexual Sex at Present,
by Discharge Status**

FREQUENCY OF HOMOSEXUAL SEX AT PRESENT	DISCHARGE STATUS	
	HD (N = 32)	LHD (N = 31)
More than once a week	47%	39%
About once a week	22	19
About once every other week	19	19
About once a month	6	12
Less often	6	10

When frequencies are combined in rows 1–2 and 3–5, $\gamma = .23$,
$z = 0.730$, two-tailed $p = .540$.

difference between our groups.

The Chicago data show that 79 percent (38) of the HD group
reported homosexual frequency of at least once a week compared
to 69 percent (22) of the LHD group. This difference is not
significant ($\gamma = -.27$, $z = -1.047$, two-tailed $p = .296$).

OVERTNESS

Respondents were asked, "To what extent do you care at the
present time that people might find out about your homosexuality?" The results are shown in Table 49. As the table shows, there
is little difference between our groups.

EXCLUSIVENESS

Respondents were asked to rate themselves as to their sexual
orientation on a modified form of the Kinsey scale. The full results of this have been presented in Table 19 of Chapter 6. From

**Table 49. Present Concern over Exposure,
by Discharge Status**

PRESENT CONCERN OVER EXPOSURE OF HOMOSEXUALITY	DISCHARGE STATUS	
	HD (N = 32)	LHD (N = 31)
Very concerned	34%	26%
Somewhat concerned	28	29
Very little concerned	22	23
Not concerned at all	16	23

When frequencies are combined in rows 1–2 and 3–4,
$\gamma = .16$, $z = 0.359$, one-tailed $p = .360$.

this we see that 63 percent (20) of the HD group defined themselves as exclusively homosexual compared to 68 percent (21) of the LHD group, the difference being statistically nonsignificant ($\gamma = -.11$, $z = 0.171$, one-tailed $p = .432$). Nearly 90 percent of both groups placed themselves in one of the top two categories (exclusively homosexual or mainly homosexual and insignificantly heterosexual).

The way in which respondents from the Chicago study rated themselves was also presented in Chapter 6 (Table 19B). Again, no significant differences appear between the HD and LHD groups.

Two other questions were asked which also reflect exclusiveness: had they ever been married and had they ever had sexual intercourse with a female. Sixteen percent (5) of the HD group had been or were married compared to 19 percent (6) of the LHD group ($\gamma = -.13$, $z = 0.057$, two-tailed $p = .954$); 81 percent (26) of the HD group compared to 68 percent (21) of the LHD group had had intercourse with a female ($\gamma = .35$, $z = 0.935$, one-tailed $p = .175$). In neither case are these differences significant.

Twenty-three percent (11) of the HD group and 13 percent (4) of the LHD group had been married among the Chicago sample. This difference is not significant ($\gamma = -.35$, $z = -1.162$, one-tailed $p = .123$). Eighty-one percent (39) of the HD group had had sexual intercourse with a female compared to 56 percent

(18) of the LHD group. The difference is significant ($\gamma = .68$, $z = 2.795$, one-tailed $p = .003$), with the HD group being more likely to have experienced heterosexual intercourse than the LHD group.

Various other indicants were examined in the consideration of involvement in the homosexual way of life which reflect the multisidedness of that life, from the number of friends the respondent has who are homosexual to the more esoteric and symbolic forms of involvement such as going in "drag" (wearing clothing of the opposite sex in public).

HOMOSEXUAL FRIENDSHIPS

Respondents were asked what proportion of all their friends were homosexual; the results appear in Table 50. As can be seen

Table 50. **Proportion of Homosexual Friends, by Discharge Status**

PROPORTION OF ALL FRIENDS WHO ARE HOMOSEXUAL	DISCHARGE STATUS	
	HD (N = 32)	LHD (N = 31)
25% and under	16%	19%
26–75%	37	39
Over 75%	47	42

When frequencies are combined in rows 1–2, $\gamma = -.10$, $z = 0.060$, two-tailed $p = .952$.

from this table, no significant difference is evident.

In the Chicago sample, 65 percent (31) of the HD group as compared to 78 percent (25) of the LHD group reported that over 75 percent of their friends were homosexual ($\gamma = -.32$, $z = -1.286$, one-tailed $p = .099$), a difference not considered significant.

Respondents were also asked the same question with regard to their close friends. The results are shown in Table 51. Again there are no significant differences. This question was not asked of Chicago respondents.

Table 51. **Proportion of Homosexual Close Friends,**
      by Discharge Status

PROPORTION OF CLOSE FRIENDS WHO ARE HOMOSEXUAL	DISCHARGE STATUS	
	HD (N = 32)	LHD (N = 31)
25% and under	12%	19%
26–75%	41	42
Over 75%	47	39

When frequencies are combined in rows 1–2, $\gamma = -.16$, $z = 0.397$,
      two-tailed $p = .692$.

LIVING WITH ANOTHER HOMOSEXUAL

Setting up a domestic relationship with another homosexual indicates another type of commitment to the homosexual way of life. The majority of respondents, 88 percent (28) for the HD group, and 87 percent (27) for the LHD group, had done this ($\gamma = .01$, $z = -0.327$, two-tailed $p = .744$); and of these, 50 percent (14) of the HD group and 63 percent (17) of the LHD group were still in such a situation ($\gamma = .26$, $z = 0.690$, one-tailed $p = .245$). These differences are not statistically significant.

HOMOSEXUAL REFERENCE GROUP

Respondents were asked how important it was to them that their *best homosexual friends* and *homosexuals in general* had a good opinion of them. Regarding the first category, 63 percent (20) of the HD group and 60 percent (18) of the LHD group said this was very important, there being no statistically significant difference between the groups ($\gamma = .05$, $z = -0.058$, two-tailed $p = .954$). For the second category, those saying very or somewhat important were 59 percent (19) and 61 percent (19), respectively, again there being no significant difference ($\gamma = -.04$, $z = -0.101$, one-tailed $p = .460$). No comparable question was asked of Chicago respondents.

We now examine three items that reflect the involvement of the homosexual in the wider homosexual subculture.

EXTENT OF HOMOSEXUAL SOCIAL ACTIVITIES

Respondents were asked about the extensity of their social activities with other homosexuals. The results appear in Table 52,

Table 52. Extent of Homosexual Social Activities at Present, by Discharge Status

EXTENT OF HOMOSEXUAL SOCIAL ACTIVITIES AT PRESENT	DISCHARGE STATUS	
	HD (N = 31)	LHD (N = 31)
Not active at all	0%	3%
Not too active	12	16
Somewhat active	35	42
Very active	52	39

When frequencies are combined in rows, 1–3, $\gamma = -.26$, $z = 0.759$, two-tailed $p = .448$.

and show that there are no significant differences between our groups

GOING IN DRAG

Wearing the clothes of the opposite sex to parties or dances is an integral part of "camping," which has been defined as characteristic of the cultural life of the homosexual community.[1] It is not our intention to explicate this phenomenon in any detailed way. Suffice it to say that it is symbolic of involvement in a segment of the homosexual community, although, of course, it is neither a necessary nor sufficient condition for such involvement. Such behavior seemed not to characterize either of our groups—only one person in the HD group and three in the LHD group.

Sixteen persons in the Chicago sample reported ever having gone in drag: 12 percent (6) of the HD group and 31 percent (10) of the LHD group. This difference is a significant difference ($\gamma = .52$, $z = 2.041$, one-tailed $p = .020$). An associated finding exists with regard to the more general expression of "camping"

---

[1] William Simon and John H. Gagnon, "Homosexuality: The Formulation of a Sociological Perspective," *Journal of Health and Social Behavior,* 8 (September 1967), 182.

behavior. The Chicago respondents were asked, "During the past year, have you acted in a campy or swishy way?" Thirty-five percent (17) of the HD group said that they had compared to 56 percent (18) of the LHD group ($\gamma = .40$, $z = 1.828$, one-tailed $p = .034$). This latter finding must be interpreted with caution in that it only refers to the last year and not "ever." However, both findings are in line with what was originally predicted.

FREQUENTING GAY BARS

The major institution of the homosexual community is the "gay bar," bars that cater almost exclusively to homosexuals and used by them as a major locale for making sexual contacts as well as serving a host of other social functions.[2] Presence in a gay bar is public evidence (at least to homosexuals) of other like-minded individuals, thus frequenting such institutions is an important indicant of a person's involvement in the homosexual world. A comparison of our groups on frequency of attendance at gay bars is shown in Table 53. There are no significant differences between our groups.

Table 53. Frequency of Attendance at Gay Bars, by Discharge Status

FREQUENCY OF ATTENDANCE AT GAY BARS	DISCHARGE STATUS	
	HD (N = 32)	LHD (N = 31)
At least once every other week or more	44%	45%
About once a month	28	19
Less often	25	16
Never	3	19

When frequencies are combined in rows 1–2 and 3–4, $\gamma = .17$, $z = 0.358$, two-tailed $p = .720$.

---

[2] For a description of the homosexual bar and its functions, see Evelyn Hooker, "The Homosexual Community," in James O. Palmer and Michael J. Goldstein (eds.), *Perspectives in Psychopathology* (New York: Oxford University Press, 1966), pp. 354–64; and Nancy Achilles, "The Development of the Homosexual Bar as an Institution," in John H. Gagnon and William Simon (eds.), *Sexual Deviance* (New York: Harper & Row, 1967), pp. 214–28.

In the Chicago sample 63 percent (30) of the HD group as against 58 percent (18) of the LHD group reported going to gay bars once a month or more over the last year. This difference is not significant ($\gamma = -.09$, $z = -0.391$, two-tailed $p = .696$).

RELATING TO THE HETEROSEXUAL WORLD

As well as increasing identification with and involvement in a deviant group, labeling theory posits increased estrangement from conventional groups and institutions on the part of the officially identified deviant. We examine this in our sample, beginning first with the extent of public knowledge about the individual's homosexuality. We refer to this variable as "known-aboutness."

KNOWNABOUTNESS

Knowledge of a less than honorable discharge is restricted with regard to the audience it reaches. The individual initially has his deviance known to military authorities and perhaps to a number of service friends and acquaintances. At any rate he is usually far from home and isolated in a military setting. Those of his peers who do find out are also unlikely to be from his specific locale or to share other nonservice relationships with him. Thus, initially, the audience to whom his deviance is known is restricted. Furthermore, after his expulsion from the military setting, he is of no further concern to those who have applied a deviant label to him. The only external scar he bears is in the form of a document, his discharge papers.

Thus, it is no great problem, as we have seen, to exercise information control and create a barrier between military and civilian worlds whereby what is known to one is not known to the other. This is not to say that this barrier is never breached; it is possible for other persons to find out about the discharge by accident, by questioning and so forth. It is a further possibility, recognized by labeling theorists, that the dischargee may voluntarily disclose this information.[3] Official labeling brings a deviant

---

[3] Voluntary disclosure is discussed by Goffman. See Erving Goffman, *Stigma: Notes on the Management of Spoiled Identity* (Englewood Cliffs, N.J.: Prentice-Hall, 1965), pp. 100–102.

face to face with the fact that his condition or behavior is condemned by society. It often occurs that such official labeling is followed by self-labeling on the part of the deviant as he comes to see himself as others see him. This can lead to extreme feelings of guilt and shame and a consequent self-punishment that often becomes "intolerable." One way of dealing with such pain is to disclose one's deviance to others upon whom one relies for comfort and support (or, as some psychologists might suggest, for punishment).

A third possibility is that the individual straightaway accepts the label and the identity implied, makes no effort at concealment, and seeks others who overtly live the life of the systematic deviant.

Whether knownaboutness occurs, therefore, from accident, "confidentiality," or display, it is likely that the person who has undergone an official labeling experience and has a "secret difference" will be more knownabout to others than the person whose deviance has not been so illuminated. Thus we would expect those homosexuals who received a less than honorable discharge from the military to be more known as homosexual than those who received Honorable Discharges. The data appear in Table 54. We designated several categories of people and asked the respondent how many people he thought in each category knew or suspected that he was homosexual. The table shows no significant differences between our groups, although the LHD group scores consistently higher in knownaboutness.

In addition to asking how knownabout our respondents thought they were to groups of people, we also asked whether they thought they were known to various individuals. Unfortunately, in some cases the person had no such relationship or said they just couldn't answer. Percentages, therefore, are computed on the basis of those who were able to answer; the number who answered each question are noted in parentheses (see Table 55).

The results show that the LHD group is more likely to report themselves as being knownabout to their fathers and employers than the HD group, all other differences being nonsignificant.

These findings receive support from the Chicago data. Con-

Table 54. Knownaboutness (Groups), by Discharge Status

RESPONDENT SCORES HIGH ON KNOWNABOUTNESS AMONG*	DISCHARGE STATUS		γ	z	one-tailed p's
	HD (N = 32)	LHD (N = 31)			
Heterosexuals he knows	31%	35%	.10	.088	.465
Male heterosexual friends	31	35	.10	.088	.465
Female heterosexual friends	31	35	.16	.354	.362
Aunts and uncles	22	42	.44	1.427	.077
Other relatives	19	29	.28	.657	.256
Neighbors	19	32	.35	.934	.175
Work associates	56	74	.38	1.219	.112
People he suspects or knows are homosexual	62	74	.27	.720	.236

* The possible responses were all, most, more than half, half, less than half, few, none. Those who answered other than few or none are here defined as scoring high on knownaboutness. For ease of presentation, only one row of percentages from each individual run are presented, the residual row being omitted.

Table 55. Knownaboutness (Specific Persons), by Discharge Status

RESPONDENTS STATE THE FOLLOWING DEFINITELY KNOW OR SUSPECT HE IS HOMOSEXUAL*	DISCHARGE STATUS				γ	z	one-tailed p's
	HD (N = 32)		LHD (N = 31)				
Mother	43%	(30)	52%	(29)	— .17	.426	.335
Father	33	(27)	62	(26)	— .52	1.764	.039
Best male heterosexual friend	61	(31)	77	(30)	— .35	1.011	.156
Best female heterosexual friend	59	(32)	71	(28)	— .27	.717	.237
Employer	14	(28)	52	(27)	— .73	2.656	.004

* For ease of presentation the residual row of percentages has been omitted. These involve those respondents who said of each individual that they do not know or suspect.

cerning knownaboutness to their fathers, 30 percent (12) of the HD group and 73 percent (19) of the LHD group said their fathers definitely knew or suspected they were homosexual ($\gamma =$ .73, $z = 3.400$, one-tailed $p = .0004$). Another difference was found which did not appear previously which concerns known-aboutness to their mothers. Forty-nine percent (22) of the HD group said their mothers knew or suspected compared to 87 percent (27) of the LHD group ($\gamma = .75$, $z = 3.397$, one-tailed $p = .0004$). There was no comparable question on employers, although respondents were asked how many co-workers knew of their homosexuality on their last full-time job. Forty-seven percent (7) of the HD group compared to 66 percent (20) of the LHD reported that their co-workers knew ($\gamma = .37$, $z = 1.638$, one-tailed $p = .051$). Finally, another difference appeared concerning how many of their male heterosexual friends knew they were homosexual: 39 percent (11) of the HD group said all or most compared to 68 percent (13) of the LHD group, again a significant difference ($\gamma = .54$, $z = 1.939$, one-tailed $p = .026$).

We can conclude this section on knownaboutness, therefore, by saying that in our sample, despite few significant differences, all relationships found were in the predicted direction. Of those findings that are statistically significant, the LHD group was more likely to report that their homosexuality was known to their fathers and their employers. These findings do not seem attributable to the fact that the LHD group was further advanced in their homosexual careers at induction as when the variable prior sex frequency was introduced the relationships still held. The Chicago results supported our knownaboutness hypotheses with the LHD group being more knownabout to their fathers, mothers, co-workers, and male heterosexual friends.

HETEROSEXUAL REFERENCE GROUP

We would expect that in the face of punishment from the heterosexual world, the officially labeled homosexual would withdraw more into the homosexual subculture or at least be less enamored with the moral codes of the heterosexual world. He has been "set apart" as undesirable; his moral worth has been devalued, and no role exists for his particular proclivity that is not a deviant one. We may expect him, therefore, to "reject the rejectors" more firmly than those deviants fortunate enough not to become enmeshed with the degradation ceremonies of the conventional world.[4]

The respondents were asked, "How important is it to you that heterosexuals in general have a good opinion of you?" The data are presented in Table 56. As the table shows, there are no sig-

Table 56. Importance of the Opinions of Heterosexuals in General, by Discharge Status

OPINIONS OF HETEROSEXUALS IN GENERAL	DISCHARGE STATUS	
	HD (N = 32)	LHD (N = 30)
Very important	34%	47%
Somewhat important	53	30
Not very important	13	20
Not at all important	0	3

When frequencies are combined in rows 2–4, $\gamma = -.25$, $z = 0.721$, two-tailed $p = .594$.

nificant differences between the two groups. No comparable question was asked of Chicago respondents.

Continuing our argument, we predicted that the officially labeled homosexual would be in a particular relationship to conventional institutions. Three selected institutions were work, politics, and religion.

WORK

As we have seen, relating to the world of work is particularly stressful for the homosexual with a less than honorable discharge. An Honorable Discharge is often the most important reference a young man has, as he is unlikely to have had much work experience prior to induction into the military. Many other jobs require security clearances and all federal and many state jobs require that applicants possess an Honorable Discharge from the military. We have seen how difficulties over employment are viewed

---

[4] Gresham M. Sykes and David Matza, "Techniques of Neutralization: A Theory of Delinquency," *American Sociological Review*, 22 (December 1957), 664–70.

by our respondents as the most important effects of an irregular discharge. We next see how those who received such discharges compare to those who did not on items concerning their employment situation at present.

Occupational level. We have already presented data on the occupational status of our respondents (Chapter 6). It will be remembered that the majority of respondents from both groups were in white-collar occupations and that within the "white-collar level" there were no differences between our groups.

Occupational mobility. Some respondents said that receiving a less than honorable discharge retarded their careers in that they were unable to obtain the occupations for which they were trained. While we had no direct measure of mobility or restricted potential, the following method was employed to give some such indication. From the census it was determined what the median annual income was for various levels of educational achievement. Next, the respondent's education and income level were compared with the median income to see if he was above it, below it, or "within" it. (We had grouped categories for income on the questionnaire; thus, for some respondents, checking a group category which included the median income for that educational level meant we could not say whether he was below or above the median. Thus he was called "at the median.") The results of this exercise were as follows (see Table 57). No significant differences appear between our groups, and no trends can be isolated.[5]

Number of jobs. Difficulty with employment can also be indicated by the number of full-time occupations held by the respondent. Comparing both our groups on the number of full-time occupations they had had since leaving school, 50 percent (16) of the HD group stated they had had three or more compared to 58 percent (18) of the LHD group. This difference is not statistically significant ($\gamma = -.16$, $z = 0.386$, one-tailed $p = .350$). A

---

[5] We recognize the crudity of this measure; e.g., the census reports on a national sample, whereas our sample is restricted to two areas, etc.

Table 57. Occupational Mobility and Potential, by Discharge Status

INCOME AS COMPARED TO EDUCATION IS:	DISCHARGE STATUS	
	HD (N = 32)	LHD (N = 31)
Above median	34%	32%
At the median	38	45
Below median	28	23

When frequencies are combined in rows 1–2, $\gamma = .05$, $z = -0.088$, two-tailed $p = .930$.

significant difference in number of occupations was found among the groups in the Chicago sample, however. Twenty-three percent (11) of the HD group reported having held more than three occupations compared to 41 percent (13) of the LHD group ($\gamma = -.39$, $z = -1.682$, one-tailed $p = .046$).

Unemployment. Respondents were asked how often since leaving school they had been unemployed and looking for work for more than thirty days. The results which follow in Table 58

Table 58. Times Unemployed, by Discharge Status

TIMES UNEMPLOYED FOR MORE THAN 30 DAYS SINCE LEAVING SCHOOL	DISCHARGE STATUS	
	HD (N = 32)	LHD (N = 31)
Never	38%	39%
1–2	34	35
3–4	19	10
5 and over	9	16

When frequencies are combined in rows 2–4, $\gamma = -.02$, $z = -0.159$, two-tailed $p = .874$.

show no statistically significant difference between the groups. This question was taken from the Chicago study; the corresponding data from that study also show no significant difference between the groups on unemployment experiences. Sixty-three percent (30) of the HD group and 53 percent (17) of the LHD group said they had "never" been unemployed ($\gamma = .19$, $z = -0.829$, one-tailed $p = .204$).

Trouble at work. Respondents were asked if they had had problems at work or lost a job because of their homosexuality becoming known. Sixteen percent (5) of the HD group compared to 26 percent (8) of the LHD group said they had lost a job for this reason ($\gamma = .31$, $z = 0.681$, one-tailed $p = .348$). Twenty-two percent (7) of the HD group and 32 percent (10) of the LHD group said, in addition, that they had experienced problems at work due to their homosexuality ($\gamma = .26$, $z = 0.639$, one-tailed $p = .262$). In both cases these differences are not statistically significant. In the Chicago sample, 8 percent (4) of the HD group compared to 19 percent (6) of the LHD group reported having trouble on a job because of homosexuality ($\gamma = .43$, $z = 1.371$, one-tailed $p = .085$). Only three respondents reported ever having lost a job because of their homosexuality: two HD group members and one LHD group member.

RELIGION

There was no difference between the two groups in estrangement from formal religion, 47 percent (15) of the HD group stating that they had no religious affiliation compared to 32 percent (10) of the LHD group ($\gamma = .30$, $z = 0.920$, two-tailed $p = .358$). In addition, 53 percent (17) of the HD group stated that they never attended church or synagogue compared to 50 percent (15) of the LHD group ($\gamma = -.06$, $z = -0.008$, two-tailed $p = .994$). Neither was there a difference in the evaluation of religion. Respondents were asked how important religion was to them; 59 percent (19) of the HD group said it was of little or no importance, compared to 45 percent (14) of the LHD group. Again the difference is not statistically significant ($\gamma = .28$, $z = 0.870$, two-tailed $p = .384$).

Religious affiliation of the Chicago sample was discussed in Chapter 6; no important differences were found between the groups in terms of affiliation. Concerning religious attendance during the past three months, 54 percent (26) of the HD group and 72 percent (23) of the LHD group said they never attended church or synagogue. This difference is considered significant ($\gamma = -.37$, $z = -1.582$, one-tailed $p = .057$). There was no difference, however, between the groups with regard to the "importance of religion" to them. Forty-four percent (21) of the HD group and 41 percent (13) of the LHD group said they were slightly or not at all religious ($\gamma = .06$, $z = 0.275$, two-tailed $p = .784$).

POLITICS

It was hypothesized that being officially labeled deviant would make a person politically active and desirous of changing the system that brands him as undesirable. Respondents were asked a set of questions on their political attitudes and behavior. First, they were asked how interested they were in national politics. Sixty-two percent (20) of the HD group said they were very much interested compared to 52 percent (16) of the LHD group, this difference being statistically nonsignificant ($\gamma = .22$, $z = 0.613$, two-tailed $p = .540$). Next, they were asked how often they voted in national or local elections. Ninety-seven percent (31) of the HD group said often as compared to 71 percent (22) of the LHD group, this difference being significant ($\gamma = .85$, $z = 2.384$, two-tailed $p = .018$) but opposite to our hypothesis. In terms of political ideology, 48 percent (15) of the HD group defined themselves as liberal compared to 40 percent (12) of the LHD group, not a significant difference ($\gamma = .16$, $z = 0.397$, two-tailed $p = .692$). No respondent defined himself politically as a radical.

Finally, we asked how active they were in the homophile organization to which they belonged. Twenty-nine percent (8) of the HD group said they were very or fairly active as compared to 27 percent (8) of the LHD group, this difference being nonsignificant ($\gamma = -.02$, $z = -0.214$, two-tailed $p = .830$).

In the Chicago sample 81 percent (39) of the HD group said they often voted in national and local elections compared to 59 percent (19) of the LHD group, a difference that was significant but again not in the direction we predicted ($\gamma = -.49$, $z = -2.133$, two-tailed $p = .034$). A related question asked how active the respondent was in politics—again, a difference appeared that was considered significant. Sixty-five percent (31) of the HD group reported that they *never* attended political meetings, rallies, and so forth, compared with 84 percent (27) of the LHD group ($\gamma =$ $- .50, z = - 1.930$, two-tailed $p = .054$). No differences appeared in "liberal" identification, however, 56 percent (27) of the HD group and 42 percent (13) of the LHD group defining themselves as liberal ($\gamma = .28, z = 1.234$, two-tailed $p = .218$). No question was asked on activity in homophile organizations. Only 25 percent (20) of the sample were homophile members, 23 percent (11) of the HD group and 28 percent (9) of the LHD group ($\gamma = .14, z = 0.523$, one-tailed $p = .300$).

Therefore, with regard to relating to conventional institutions, we find little difference between our groups. Few of the percentage differences are large, and no consistent findings appear as regards direction of the differences. Prior sex frequency was introduced in an attempt at specification, but as previously mentioned these tables are not presented or discussed, as the introduction of this variable had no significant effect.

PERSONAL AND PSYCHOLOGICAL ADJUSTMENT

We mentioned earlier the assumed psychic costs of being labeled deviant. If deviance is handled by duplicity, the efforts at information control and the fear of exposure can cause strain. On the other hand, opting to live disclosed as a deviant can cause problems in the face of hostile reactions (real or imagined) from the conventional world. In either case, such strains may be reacted to in ways that cause further problems. We predicted, therefore, that those homosexuals less than honorably discharged from the military would show more signs of personal and psychological maladjustment than those who were honorably discharged. Comparing our groups on various indices of adjustment gave us the following results.

USE OF ALCOHOL

Respondents were first asked how often they went out drinking, with the results shown in Table 59. No significant differences appear between the groups.

Since frequency of going out drinking is neither a necessary nor sufficient condition for a drinking problem, respondents were

Table 59. Frequency of Drinking, by Discharge Status

FREQUENCY OF GOING OUT DRINKING	DISCHARGE STATUS	
	HD (N = 32)	LHD (N = 30)
Four or more times a week	3%	3%
One to three times a week	16	23
About once every two weeks	25	17
About once a month	19	17
Less often	22	23
Never	16	17

When frequencies are combined in rows 1–4 and 5–6, $\gamma = .05$, $z = -0.058$, two-tailed $p = .954$.

asked how they classified themselves as drinkers. The results are shown in Table 60. Again no significant difference appears between the groups.

Table 60. Drinking Status, by Discharge Status

RESPONDENT CLASSIFIED HIMSELF AS:	DISCHARGE STATUS	
	HD (N = 32)	LHD (N = 31)
A nondrinker	6%	16%
An occasional drinker	44	32
A moderate drinker	37	48
A heavy drinker	13	3

When frequencies in rows 1–2 and 3–4 are combined, $\gamma = .03$, $z = -0.123$, one-tailed $p = .451$.

In the Chicago sample, 58 percent (28) of the HD group and 63 percent (20) of the LHD group classified themselves as moderate or heavy drinkers, this being a nonsignificant difference ($\gamma = -.09$, $z = -0.370$, one-tailed $p = .356$).

The final question in this set asked, "How often in the last year have you drunk enough so that you felt high?" Responses to this question were as shown in Table 61. There is little difference between the groups.

No significant difference on this item was found for the Chicago sample either. Forty-five percent (19) of the HD group and 50

Table 61. Frequency of Getting High on Alcohol (in the last year), by Discharge Status

FREQUENCY OF GETTING HIGH ON ALCOHOL	DISCHARGE STATUS	
	HD (N = 32)	LHD (N = 31)
More than once a week	25%	26%
More than once a month	19	19
Less often	41	35
Never	16	19

When frequencies are combined in rows 1–2 and 3–4, $\gamma = -.03$, $z = -0.140$, one-tailed $p = .444$.

percent (15) of the LHD group said they only got "high" on special occasions or not at all ($\gamma = -.04$, $z = -0.210$, two-tailed $p = .834$).

USE OF DRUGS

Respondents were asked if they had regularly used sleeping pills, pep pills, or tranquilizers. In response, 19 percent (6) of the HD group admitted to this compared to 29 percent (8) of the LHD group, this difference being too small for statistical significance ($\gamma = -.20$, $z = 0.367$, one-tailed $p = .356$).

SUICIDE

The question asked was if the respondent had ever seriously considered suicide. Thirty-eight percent (12) of the HD group answered Yes compared to 58 percent (18) of the LHD group; this difference, though quite large, does not reach our stipulated level of statistical significance ($\gamma = -.40$, $z = 1.370$, one-tailed $p = .085$).

Concerning attempted suicide, 9 percent (3) of the HD group had attempted suicide compared with 32 percent (10) of the LHD group; this difference is also not significant ($\gamma = -.64$, $z = 0.606$, one-tailed $p = .272$).

For the Chicago sample there is a significant difference in connection with suicide consideration. Twenty-nine percent (14) of the HD group reported that they had considered suicide as against 63 percent (20) of the LHD group ($\gamma = .60$, $z = 2.936$, one-tailed $p = .002$). In addition, a similar difference that is statistically significant appeared for those attempting suicide; 10 percent (5) of the HD group had attempted suicide compared to 50 percent (16) of the LHD group ($\gamma = -.79$, $z = 3.659$, one-tailed $p = .0006$).

DEPRESSION

Two items were used to examine the respondent's depression: the first one asked how happy he was; the second, how much fun he got out of life. Ninety-one percent (29) of the HD group said they were very or fairly happy compared to 88 percent (27) of the LHD group (the other possible responses being "not very happy" and "very unhappy"). This difference is not statistically significant ($\gamma = .18$, $z = 0.044$, one-tailed $p = .482$). Seventy-five percent (24) of the HD group strongly agreed or agreed with the statement, "I get a lot of fun out of life," compared with 84 percent (26) of the LHD group (other responses being disagree and strongly disagree). Again this difference is not statistically significant ($\gamma = -.27$, $z = 0.554$, two-tailed $p = .580$).

In the Chicago study, 92 percent (44) of the HD group reported that they were very happy or pretty happy as compared with 72 percent (23) of the LHD group. Although this is a significant difference ($\gamma = -.62$, $z = -2.336$, one-tailed $p = .010$), it should be noted that the majority of respondents did report that they were more likely to be happy than not. (The third possible response was "Not too happy.")

GUILT, SHAME, ANXIETY

These questions were designed to find out the respondent's attitude toward his homosexuality. The first question asked was, "Does knowing you are homosexual 'weigh on your mind' (make you feel guilty, depressed, anxious or ashamed)?" The results are shown in Table 62. As can be seen from the table, there are few differences, none of which approaches statistical significance.

The next question asked respondents if they experienced shame, guilt, or anxiety after having homosexual relations. Seventy-five percent (24) of the HD group said "never" as compared

Table 62. Feelings of Guilt and Shame About Being Homosexual, by Discharge Status

DOES KNOWING YOU ARE HOMOSEXUAL "WEIGH ON YOUR MIND" (MAKE YOU FEEL GUILTY, ANXIOUS OR ASHAMED)?	DISCHARGE STATUS	
	HD (N = 32)	LHD (N = 31)
A great deal	0%	10%
Somewhat	13	6
Not very much	38	29
Not at all	50	55

When frequencies are combined in rows 1–3, $\gamma = .10$, $z = 0.131$, two-tailed $p = .896$.

with 68 percent (21) of the LHD group (the other responses being always, often, not often); this is not a statistically significant difference ($\gamma = .18$, $z = 0.356$, one-tailed $p = .361$).

Respondents were also asked to check items on a psychosomatic checklist that measures anxiety symptoms.[6] They were asked how often certain things happened to them (for example, nightmares, dizzy spells, etc.), and each respondent received a total score on the scale. There were 15 items on the scale, and respondents could check: nearly all the time, pretty often, not very much, or never. These responses were scored from 4 to 1 so that the highest possible score was 60 and the lowest was 15. The

Table 63. Anxiety Symptoms, by Discharge Status

ANXIETY SCORE	DISCHARGE STATUS	
	HD (N = 32)	LHD (N = 31)
Low (15–22)	16%	35%
(23–37)	84	61
(38–52)	0	3
High (53–60)	0	0

When frequencies in rows 2–4 are combined, $\gamma = -.50$, $z = 1.508$, two-tailed $p = .132$.

---

[6] This scale comes from Morris Rosenberg, *Society and the Adolescent Self-Image* (Princeton, N.J.: Princeton University Press, 1965). The scale is reproduced in Appendix 4 of the present book.

results obtained from this scale are shown in Table 63. As can be seen from this table, there was little dispersion in scores. There is no significant difference between the HD and LHD groups.

The Chicago study also utilized a psychosomatic checklist indicative of psychological maladjustment. Although the items included in it were not identical to ours (though they were similar), the results obtained are interesting in that they correspond to the unanticipated direction of the difference found in our sample. Respondents were scored on the checklist and the sample divided into those who showed "high," "medium," or "low" maladjustment. Forty percent (19) of the HD group were found to be highly maladjusted compared to only 16 percent (5) of the LHD group, a difference that is statistically significant and which is opposite again to what we predicted ($\gamma = -.56$, $z = -2.276$, two-tailed $p = .024$).

In conclusion, few differences appeared between our groups in "objective" characteristics. Two differences did appear, however. First, the LHD group reported more knownaboutness, and second, the LHD group was shown to be less politically active than the HD group in that they voted less often in local and national elections. This finding is contrary to our predictions.

Further differences appeared in the Chicago study.

1. Those supportive of our findings: The LHD group was found to be more knownabout to their fathers and to participate less in politics than the HD group.

2. Those supportive of our hypotheses: Members of the LHD group were also found to be more knownabout to their mothers, co-workers, and male heterosexual friends than were members of the HD group. They were also found to have "considered" suicide more and to have attempted suicide more. In addition, compared to the HD group, the LHD group was found:

(a) to be less likely to have had sexual intercourse with a female
(b) to be more likely to "camp" or have gone in "drag"
(c) to have had more occupations

    (d) to have attended religious functions less (in the three
          months prior to the interview)
    (e) to score lower in happiness

3. Those contradicting our hypotheses: The LHD group was found to vote less often and to be less active in politics than the HD group. Finally, the LHD group among the Chicago sample was found to score lower on psychological maladjustment than the HD group.

Chapter 12

SUMMARY AND CONCLUSION

This research has examined one instance of official labeling: less than honorable discharge from the military for reasons that concern homosexuality. In organizing the research, the theoretical perspective known as the labeling approach was adopted. It appeared that this was an opportunity to examine some of its more general tenets; in no strict sense, however, was this research to be considered a "test of labeling theory."

The two central questions that guided the research were:

1. What are the processes whereby a person comes to be labeled homosexual by military authorities? To what extent does his own behavior contribute to his being labeled?

2. What are the consequences of being officially labeled, of leaving the military with a less than honorable discharge? What are the effects upon a person's perception of himself and others now that he has been adjudged "undesirable"? What are the consequences regarding his life chances, his deviant career, and his relationship to the conventional world?

In answering these questions, we compared a sample of homosexuals who had received less than honorable discharges from the military (LHD group) with a sample of homosexuals who had served in the military but had received Honorable Discharges (HD group). The results obtained are discussed below. Whenever possible, replication was attempted, with data gathered in Chicago by the Institute for Sex Research.

In answer to the first question, it was found that the LHD group came to the attention of military authorities usually in one of three ways: (a) being informed upon directly or indirectly, (b) by voluntarily admitting that they were homosexual, or (c) through their own indiscretion.

Comparing the LHD group to the HD group, several factors were suggested as playing a role in why the former group had their deviance discovered and the latter group did not. The first of these referred to how advanced the respondent was in his homosexual career prior to his induction into the military. Evidence was provided to show that the LHD group experienced higher frequencies of homosexual sex at the time of their induction than did the HD group. The second factor involved the characteristics of the respondent's homosexual interactions while he was in the military. Members of the LHD group reported more frequent homosexual sex while in the military than did members of the HD group. Third, the less than honorable dischargees were more likely to report having other servicemen as their usual sexual partners during their period of service than did members of the HD group.

The Chicago replication only supported the third of our findings, concerning whether sexual partners were usually other servicemen or not.

The original hypotheses were made more meaningful when *manner of discovery* was taken into account. We concluded that there are three main patterns which lead to the discovery of homosexuals by the military.

1. Those caught through their own indiscretion. These cases showed low frequencies of sex while in service, yet all had engaged in sex primarily with other servicemen and were *not* high in their sexual frequencies prior to induction. It was suggested that these cases contributed to discovery through inexperience in a deviant role.

2. Those voluntarily admitting their homosexuality. These cases reported low frequencies of sex while in the military, yet had high frequencies prior to induction. Their disclosure was motivated by a desire to leave the military; being further advanced in their homosexual careers apparently accounting for their relative lack of concern over the stigma of their discharge.

3. Those discovered through another person. These cases differ from the above in showing high frequencies of sex while in the

military. This pattern of discovery was most common to our respondents and represents those who put themselves more at risk regarding discovery by military authorities.

We hope to have thus shown that discovery exhibits certain patterns and does not *necessarily* involve arbitrary selection procedures by the military. Members of our sample did not appear to have suffered from a "bum rap" in that, regardless of the propriety of these rules, they had engaged in a type of behavior which, as members of a certain social system, was expressly proscribed. We are not saying that "bum raps" do not occur; rather, that in our sample proscribed behavior was engaged in by many in such a way as to lead to their being officially labeled as deviant. Therefore, it seems that in the case of this particular deviance-producing situation, the examination of the deviant himself is as important as the social control system that he offends.

The role of the military itself is of prime importance in looking at what happens to the homosexual serviceman after he is discovered. Here we saw that the traumatic effects of being discovered, plus the methods used to gain a confession, help the military to dispose of homosexuals with little difficulty.

The second central question referred to the consequences of receiving a less than honorable discharge. We looked for two main effects. The first, which we called subjective effects, involved the way in which the deviant typified himself and others as a result of being officially labeled undesirable. The second, which we called objective effects, involved his behavior, the extent and nature of his social relationships, and the like. If the discharge did have an effect, then the LHD group should be different from the HD group in certain predicted ways.

First, however, we directly asked the LHD group how they had been affected by their discharge. From their replies it seemed that in most cases the effects were short-lived, centering mainly on employment difficulties. Those who said the discharge had little or no effect were persons in certain of the professions or who had jobs that did not require an Honorable Dis-

charge from the military as part of their credentials. Those who
said the discharge had effects upon their employment were (a)
persons who had problems initially getting employment after discharge, but who eventually found satisfactory jobs after which
their discharge was no problem, and (b) persons who by their
qualifications or experience had to have security clearances and/
or desired employment in federal or local government jobs. For
this group the effects of discharge were more enduring in that
they could not take advantage of their skills or experience and
often were working in jobs they disliked.

A second major effect described by many in the LHD group
was a feeling of injustice over the way they had been treated by
the military.

With regard to the subjective effects of the discharge (attributed because of differences found between HD and LHD
responses), few differences appeared. The LHD group were
more likely to deny that homosexuals could be changed to exclusive heterosexuals than the HD group and also more likely to
believe that being homosexual made them more knowledgeable
about life in general. No corroboration for these differences appeared in the Chicago data. Though there were few direct or
indirect comparisons with the Chicago data concerning subjective differences, the results obtained were supportive in that few
differences were found between HD and LHD groups. Two
differences that did appear in the Chicago data were that the
LHD group saw more things about themselves that they would
like to change than did the HD group, and also saw more differences between homosexuals and heterosexuals; both differences
were in the direction hypothesized.

With regard to objective differences between the HD and
LHD groups the following were found. First, the members of the
LHD group were more likely to report that they were knownabout as being homosexual (specifically, to their fathers and
employers) than were members of the HD group. This can be attributed to one or both of two things. The individual's family and
other associates could have discovered his homosexuality directly as a result of the discharge. Either by an investigation

carried out in his hometown or by the curtailment of his service time, suspicion could be aroused and questions asked, resulting in the admission of his homosexuality. Although this did occur in a few cases, we feel this is limited as an explanation. Another explanation is the pressure that can ensue from having a secret differentness that is a matter of public record. The person does not know when this knowledge will appear and discredit him. Thus, in order to gain control of the situation, it is possible that he reveals his deviance to others in situations where he can have some control over the effects of such disclosure.

These findings were given support from the Chicago replication. The LHD group reported being more knownabout to their fathers, mothers, co-workers, and male heterosexual friends than did the HD group.

The second objective difference that appeared between our groups was that the LHD group voted less often in national and local elections than the HD group. This was contrary to our predictions but was replicated by the Chicago study. In addition, other items from the Chicago study indicated less political participation by the LHD group.

A final difference we consider important (because of the large percentage differences) is that the LHD group was more likely to have considered and attempted suicide than the HD group. Although these differences were not significant for our sample, in the Chicago replication they were highly significant.[1]

Other significant differences appeared in the Chicago data that were in the direction of our hypotheses. The over-all findings, however, were not of a consistency to vitiate our conclusion that while less than honorable discharge may be very traumatic in the short-term, *generally* its long-term effects for the majority of respondents are not readily apparent.

How might we explain this? Two explanations are offered, the first centering on the methodology employed.

The lack of differences could be a function of the way the

---

[1] The interviews from our sample show that most of the LHD suicide considerations and attempts occurred around the time of their separation from the military.

sample was selected. In the first place, members of the HD group were advanced enough in their homosexual careers to be in the sample. That is, they do identify enough as homosexuals to have their names on a mailing list of a homophile organization. The HD group, therefore, is probably not particularly representative of homosexuals who serve in the military and are separated with Honorable Discharges.

In the second place, the LHD group is similarly biased. That is, some persons who receive less than honorable discharges may limit their deviance as a result of the punishment they receive. This would be an argument put forward by some of the traditional social control theorists. Thus, the sampling method employed would not reach this type of person. We feel that this is a less serious criticism than the one concerning the HD group, however, because of what we know about the nature of homosexuality itself (that is, the persistence of sexual orientation).

We are comparing, therefore, two groups who are already involved in systematic deviance, and as such we are stacking the cards against labeling theory. It might be the case that if we had obtained true representative samples of the groups we are interested in, more of the differences we expected might have appeared.

The second explanation of why predicted differences did not appear is that the conception from which we made our predictions could be at fault. As we have previously mentioned, because of its unsystematic state, it is difficult to make precise predictions from labeling theory. As it stands, it is too "simple" and fails to do justice to the complexities of deviance. The present research has provoked the following thoughts on labeling theory as it stands, and its use in the elucidation of deviance.

First, despite lip service to the idea that deviance is the product of the *interaction* between labelers and those labeled deviant, most research (including ours) utilizing the perspective seems to pay attention to either one side or the other of the equation, paying less attention to the interaction itself. This is partially due, we feel, to the lack of an adequate methodology to handle the dynamics of such interaction. Labeling theory draws its main strength from symbolic interactionist theory in sociology. This school of sociology has suffered from a relative lack of empirical work, the main reason being the difficulty researchers have faced in translating the theory into empirical terms. We feel that for labeling theory in particular, more work should be done on specifying the nature and types of interaction that characterize labelers and deviants and in developing a methodology that comes to grips with the unfolding, emergent, and dynamic nature of such processes.

We need also to do more justice to the complexities of the components in the deviance-producing equation. More attention should be paid to the following:

1. *The nature of the deviant label.* Some deviant labels are more widespread in their consequences than others, and this should be recognized. In our case, it seems that less than honorable discharge was restricted in its effects; in other words, the mere fact that a person is officially labeled deviant does not tell us much unless we know the nature of the label and its disruptive potential for those who carry it. With regard to this latter point, we need to know the conditions under which the stigmatic potential of deviant labels is realized. For the majority of respondents, managing the stigma of their discharge did not pose insurmountable problems. This we feel is due mainly to the nature of the label itself having little influence outside of certain occupations and appearing on the official records of few of the organizations that circumscribe a person's life.

2. *The nature of the labelers.* It is also necessary to know more about those organizations or persons engaged in defining and processing the deviant. In connection with the previous point, it is important to know the publicity given the labeling and the extent of the interconnectedness of organizations of social control —that is, whether there is a communication network (formal or informal) whereby the knowledge of a person's deviance held by one such organization is passed on to another. In the case of the military, it was shown that publicity was not evident and information on deviants was seldom passed on to other official agen-

cies as a matter of course. Consequently, not all official labeling represents *public* labeling.

3. *The nature of the deviant and his deviance.* One of the major aims of this study was to examine the role played by the rule breaker himself in being labeled deviant. As was suggested, this is of crucial importance, neglect of which has led many investigators to see the deviant as a "victim" of the operations of social control agencies. We hope research has shown that attention should be paid to the role that the deviant plays in the labeling process. In addition to this, we feel that an important limiting condition to labeling theory as a general theory might reside in the particular deviant behavior in question. What we would suggest is that labeling by others might have extensive effects upon some forms of deviance but relatively little effect on certain aspects of other forms of deviance. It is tentatively suggested that this may be true for homosexuals as well as, for example, aspects of the behavior of drug addicts. That is, the simple problem of "supply" can lead addicts, as well as homosexuals, into subcultural involvement, leading to results (change in self-image, etc.) similar to those specified by labeling theory.

4. *Temporal features.* Labeling theory deals with the problems caused by labeling as well as with their resolution (e.g., through subcultural or group participation). Consequently, when the investigator comes on the scene, and what segment of the theory he links into, is crucial. Studying similarly labeled deviants at different points in their deviant careers, one can arrive at opposite hypotheses that follow from the labeling perspective (e.g., regarding self-acceptance). For instance, the newly labeled homosexual, according to one part of the theory, is subject to low self-acceptance, etc., whereas the labeled homosexual who has resolved identity problems by involvement in the homosexual subculture, according to another part of the theory, would be a self-accepting systematic deviant. Thus, not only is the labeling conception not fully realized as a theory, as we previously mentioned, but even where its theoretical implications seem to be clear and simple their testing can be a complex matter.

It should be recognized, therefore, that the consequences of labeling are varied and can be either positive, negative, or neutral. Being labeled deviant can have positive effects for the secret deviant in that it can resolve his problems of identity. Furthermore, he can use his self-label to get a social label which from his point of view has positive consequences—those homosexuals relatively advanced in their homosexual careers prior to induction who admitted their homosexuality in order to get out of the military are a case in point. The negative consequences of being labeled deviant have been outlined throughout and are very real. In our research, such consequences were especially experienced by those persons who cannot work at jobs they were trained for because of the discharge they received. Also, it should be recognized that labeling can have neutral consequences in that no lasting effects are forthcoming. This seemed to be the case for the majority of our sample.

It seems, therefore, that labeling theory has not lived up to its promise, and this is mainly due to the fact that it is an over-simplified conception. The revitalization of the theory by Becker was widely accepted as an antidote to current reified models of deviant behavior. Yet, reification seems to be the fate of labeling theory itself. Lemert's original presentation of the theory involved two elements: (a) the idea of social reaction to deviance—its sociological element—and (b) the idea of socialization to deviance through the production of secondary deviance and deviant self-concept—its social psychological element. The first element has been relatively neglected, whereas the second element has been trivialized. Labeling theory often has been reduced to a theory of stigma determinism, of people locked into deviant careers, never to escape. If the labeling approach is to continue to excite sociologists, the intricacies of social reality must be faced—its social psychological aspect must increase in sophistication, and its sociological aspect must be extended to fulfill its most important promise.

EPILOGUE

Regardless of the effects of less than honorable discharge, military policy concerning homosexuals is in our view unwise, unjust, and in essence unenforceable. Such policies are based on stereotypes of the homosexual that research has shown to be untenable and that result in discrimination against a minority. Not only is the cost of training lost when a serviceman is separated for homosexual conduct, but the expenditure on investigation and separation itself seems hardly worthwhile. The majority of homosexuals who serve do so with honor, and it seems foolish to pursue this group with the ardor that authorities exhibit. If an individual's sex life does not interfere with his service activities, it should be of no concern to military authorities. If it is of such a type that causes problems, then homosexuals should be separated but not necessarily in a way that is punitive. Punitiveness should be based on the nature of the offense without regard to the serviceman's sexual orientation. The automatic use of less than honorable discharges in the military's disposition of homosexuals is in our eyes immoral.

APPENDIXES

APPENDIX 1

We are engaged, with the cooperation of the Mattachine Society/SIR, in studying certain life experiences undergone by homosexuals. It would be very much appreciated if you would complete this short questionnaire (males only, please). A return envelope is provided. Please be assured that all replies will be treated in the strictest confidence. Many thanks for your assistance.

PLEASE CIRCLE THE NUMBER OPPOSITE THE
ANSWER YOU CHOOSE OR CHECK THE
APPROPRIATE RESPONSE.

1. What is your date of birth?
   _____mth. _____yr.
2. What type of work do you usually do? (be specific)
3. What was your income from all sources over the last year?
   Less than $3,000 1
   $3,000–$4,999 2
   $5,000–$7,999 3
   $8,000–$9,999 4
   $10,000–$14,999 5
   $15,000–$24,999 6
   $25,000–$49,999 7
   $50,000 and over 8
4. How far have you gone in your education?
   8th grade or less 1
   Some high school 2
   High School diploma 3
   Some college 4
   College degree 5
   Graduate degree 6

5. What is your religious background?
   Protestant 1
   Catholic 2
   Jewish 3
   Other 4
6. What kind of work does (did) your father do? (be specific)
7. What is (was) the average yearly income of your family? (mother and father)
   Less than $3,000 1
   $3,000–$4,999 2
   $5,000–$7,999 3
   $8,000–$9,999 4
   $10,000–$14,999 5
   $15,000–$24,999 6
   $25,000–$49,999 7
   $50,000 and over 8
8. What is your race?
   White 1
   Negro 2
   Other 3

191

9. Have you ever been married?
Yes_____ No_____
If YES, how old were you when you were married?
Age_____
Are you presently married?
Yes_____ No_____

10. Are you a member of the Mattachine Society/S.I.R.?
Yes_____ No_____
If YES, how old were you when you joined? Age_____

11. At what age did you have your first homosexual orgasm?
Age_____
At what age did you begin to *regularly* seek partners for homosexual relations?
Age_____
At what age did you come to think of yourself as a homosexual? (if at all)
Age_____

12. How old were you the first time someone found out about your homosexuality whom you really did not want to know?
Age_____
What was your relationship to this person?
Spouse 1
Parent 2
Brother or Sister 3
A relative 4
A friend 5
A neighbor or someone
from your community ...6
Someone at work 7
Other 8

13. Have you ever served in the armed forces?
Yes_____ No_____
(if NO, go to question 16)
If YES, in which branch did you serve?

U.S. Army 1
U.S. Navy 2
U.S. Air Force 3
U.S. Marines 4
U.S. Coast Guard 5
U.S. Merchant Marines 6
FROM: _____mth. _____yr.
TO: _____mth. _____yr.

14. If you answered YES to the above question, what type of discharge did you receive?
Honorable 1
General 2
Undesirable 3
Medical 4
Bad Conduct 5
Dishonorable 6
If your discharge was *other* than honorable, was this connected with homosexuality?

15. At the time of your induction into the armed forces, what proportion of your friends were homosexual?
None 1
Under 10% 2
10–25% 3
26–50% 4
51–75% 5
Over 75% 6
At the time of your induction into the armed forces, how extensive were your homosexual activities?
Not active at all 1
Not too active 2
Somewhat active 3
Very active 4
At the time of your induction into the armed forces, how often did you hang around with gay people?
At least once a week 1
About once every other
week 2

About once a month 3
About once every 2–5
  months 4
About once every 6–12
  months 5
Less often 6
Never 7
At the time of your induction
into the armed forces, did you
think of yourself as
  Exclusively homosexual ...1
  Mainly homosexual and
    insignificantly hetero-
    sexual 2
  Mainly homosexual and
    significantly hetero-
    sexual 3
  Equally homosexual and
    heterosexual 4
  Mainly heterosexual and
    significantly homo-
    sexual 5
  Mainly heterosexual and
    insignificantly homo-
    sexual 6
  Exclusively heterosexual ...7
At the time of your induction
into the armed forces, to what
extent did you care that people
might find out about your
homosexuality?
  Very concerned 1
  Somewhat concerned 2
  Very little concerned 3
  Not concerned at all 4
At the time of your induction
into the armed forces, were you
having homosexual sex
  More than once a week ...1
  About once a week 2
  About once every other
    week 3
  About once a month 4
  About once every 2–5
    months 5

About once every 6–12
  months 6
Less often 7
Never 8
16. Have you had any encounters
with the police concerning your
homosexuality?
Yes_____ No_____
(if NO go to question 18)
If YES, how old were you the
first time this happened?
          Age_____
Has this happened more than
once?
Yes_____ No_____
Were you ever dealt with in-
formally?
Yes_____ No_____
If YES, was this for your first
encounter_____
A subsequent encounter_____
Both_____
Were you ever "booked"?
Yes_____ No_____
If YES, was this for your first
encounter_____
A subsequent encounter_____
Both_____
Did you ever appear in court?
Yes_____ No_____
If YES, was this for your first
encounter_____
A subsequent encounter_____
Both_____
What was the most serious
charge against you?
Was this in connection with
your first encounter_____
A subsequent encounter_____
Both_____
What was your most severe
sentence?
Was this for your first encoun-
ter_____

A subsequent encounter_____
Both_____
How old were you when your most severe police case occurred?

     Age_____

Was this in connection with your first encounter_____
A subsequent encounter_____
Both_____
Has anyone ever found out about your encounters with the police?
Yes_____ No_____
If YES, who was this person?

Spouse 1
Parent 2
Brother or sister 3
Relative 4
Friend 5
Someone in your
   community 6
Someone at work 7

Did this occur at the time of your first encounter_____
A subsequent encounter_____
Both_____

17. At the time of your first police encounter, regarding your homosexuality, what proportion of your friends were homosexual?

None 1
Under 10% 2
10–25% 3
26–50% 4
51–75% 5
Over 75% 6

At the time of your first police encounter, how extensive were your homosexual activities?

Not active at all 1
Not too active 2
Somewhat active 3
Very active 4

At the time of your first police encounter, how often did you hang around with gay people?

At least once a week 1
About every other week ...2
About once a month 3
About once every
  2–5 months 4
About once every
  6–12 months 5
Less often 6
Never 7

At the time of your first police encounter, did you think of yourself as

Exclusively homosexual ...1
Mainly homosexual and
  insignificantly
  heterosexual 2
Mainly homosexual and
  significantly
  heterosexual 3
Equally homosexual and
  heterosexual 4
Mainly heterosexual and
  insignificantly
  homosexual 5
Mainly heterosexual and
  insignificantly
  homosexual 6
Exclusively heterosexual ..7

To what extent did you care at this time that people might find out about your homosexuality?

Very concerned 1
Somewhat concerned 2
Very little concerned 3
Not concerned at all 4

At the time of your first police encounter did you have homosexual sex

More than once a week ...1
About once a week 2
About once every other
  week 3
About once a month 4

About once every
2–5 months 5

About once every
6–12 months 6

Less often 7

Never 8

18. Have you ever seen a professional person about your homosexuality?

Yes_____ No_____

If YES, who was this person?

A psychiatrist 1

A psychologist 2

A physician 3

A minister, priest,
or rabbi 4

Other (specify) 5

19. Have you seen a *psychiatrist* for reasons *other* than your homosexuality?

Yes_____ No_____

If YES, how old were you the first time you did this?

Age_____

Thank you very much for answering these questions. We would like to get further information from you which cannot easily be obtained by a questionnaire. If this is acceptable, we would like the opportunity to interview you. It is important for the study that we get as many interviews as possible.

If you would give us permission for this, please provide us with your name and address so that we can contact you. Again, let us assure you that everything will be kept *confidential*.

Name:_____

Address:_____

_____

Phone:_____

Time when you are most easily reached by phone: _____

APPENDIX 2

INTERVIEW QUESTIONS

(*Part I of the Interview*)

In the administration of the interview the questions did not appear in the order they do below. Rather, they have been grouped underneath the concept for which they act as indicants. Position in the interview is signified by the number that precedes them. No probes are included.

Typification of Self
  a) Self-acceptance:
      6. In general, what do you think of yourself? What kind of person do you think you are?
      7. Do you like the kind of person you are?
      12. If there were a magic pill that would make you completely and permanently heterosexual, would you take such a pill today?
  b) Self as determined:
      9. What do you think led you to become homosexual? Do you think it was inevitable that you became a homosexual?
      10. Have you ever tried to curb your homosexual tendencies?
      11. Do you think it is possible to change homosexuals (to exclusive heterosexuality)?
  c) Self as normal:
      1. Compared to most heterosexuals you know, in what ways do you differ from them (apart from sexual orientation)?
      3. Do you think most people have both homosexual and heterosexual orientations?
      4. What proportion of homosexuals you have met do you think are psychologically disturbed? Do you think *you* are psychologically disturbed?
      5. What proportion of heterosexuals you have met do you think are psychologically disturbed?
  d) Self as a practical methodologist:

13. Do you think that being homosexual has made you more knowledgeable about life in general?

e) Sense of exposure:

17. In day-to-day situations do you think that it is easy for people to tell that you are homosexual?

18. Can other homosexuals tell without you doing something special?

Typification of Others

a) Reciprocity of perspectives:

21. What do most "straight" people think of homosexuals?

23. To what extent do you think that "straight" people realize what it's like to be a homosexual in this society?

b) Sense of injustice:

19. To what extent do you think homosexuals are themselves to blame for the reaction society has toward them?

22. In general, how do you react to "straight" people?

The following instructions regarding probing were given interviewers and referred to every question asked as well as to most questions in Part II of the interview.

1) Probe when it is necessary to get an answer to the question.

2) Probe to find out exactly what the respondent means.

3) In general, for every answer, use the following probes:

    i. What do you mean by that? (Especially when he uses general terms.)

    ii. Why do you think that, or why did you do that?

    iii. Can you tell me more about that? (Especially probe for personal experiences or detailed account of what happened.)

These probes were designed (a) to discover the categories in which the person organizes his experiences—his set of typifications, and, (b) to reveal the presuppositions underlying these typifications, especially the rules of interpretation he employs.

APPENDIX 3

MILITARY EXPERIENCES
(*Part II of the Interview*)

1. *Questions asked all respondents:*
    42. i. How old were you when you entered the forces?
        ii. Did you voluntarily enlist or were you drafted?
        iii. What was your highest pay grade in the service?
        iv. What was the highest rank you held?
    43. What type of discharge did you get?
    44. If your discharge was other than honorable, did this have anything to do with your homosexuality?
    54/67. Who knew you were homosexual *while* you were in the armed forces (if applicable)?
    55/66. iv. Compared to the time *before* you entered the forces, did you have more or less homosexual sex while you were in service (if applicable)?
    56/68. Do you think your experiences in the forces did anything to affect your homosexuality?
    57/71. How enjoyable was service life for you?
    65/72. Is there anything else that I should know about your service experiences that is important?

2. *Similar questions, different forms:*
    a) LHD Group. 59. Did you have any prior disciplinary actions against you (or get into any trouble) other than those which led to your discharge?
       HD Group. 69. Did you ever get into any trouble in the forces?
    b) LHD Group. 55. Tell me about all your homosexual activities in the services?
       HD Group. 66i. Did you engage in any homosexual activities while you were in the forces? Tell me about them.

199

3. *Questions asked LHD group only:*
    45. Tell me the circumstances of your discharge?
        a) Were you caught or did you voluntarily request it?
        b) If REQUEST, why did you request it?
        c) If CAUGHT,   i. How were you discovered? Who discovered you?
                        ii. What were you (had you been) doing?
                       iii. Who were your partner(s)?
                        iv. Where did this take place?
                         v. Were you aware of the consequences of engaging in homosexual sex?
    46. Who investigated the case?
           i. Were your personal effects searched?
          ii. Were you investigated back home?
         iii. Were you threatened or promised anything?
          iv. Were you aware of your rights?
    47. Before whom did you appear (Board of Officers, Court Martial) or did you waive your rights (sign a confession)? What happened? (If CONFESSED, why?)
    48. Did you see a psychiatrist?
    50. Did you have counsel? What were you advised?
    51. Did you go to a special unit while awaiting discharge? How long were you there? What duties did you do?
    52. About how long was it from the beginning of your investigation till your final separation?
    53. Tell me what happened while you were waiting for your discharge? How were you treated?
    58. Would you have liked to remain in the service?
    60. Has getting a less than honorable discharge affected your life at all? In what ways? What are your feelings about getting this discharge?
    61. Have you lost (or been refused) any jobs on account of your discharge?
    62. Are there any jobs for which you are qualified, and which you would like to take, but which you cannot for reasons concerning your discharge?
    63. After discharge did you return to your own hometown? If NO, why not? If YES, did local authorities know of your discharge?
    64. Have you ever attempted to appeal the conditions of your discharge? If NO, why not? If YES, how soon after was this? What was the outcome? If APPEAL DENIED, do you intend to appeal again?

APPENDIX 4

QUESTIONNAIRE 2

PLEASE CIRCLE THE NUMBER OPPOSITE THE ANSWER
THAT YOU CHOOSE OR CHECK THE APPROPRIATE
RESPONSE.

1. How many different kinds of full time occupations have you had since you left school?

2. Since leaving school, how often have you been unemployed and looking for work for more than 30 days?

3. How long has been your longest stretch of not working (other than for illnesses)?

4. Have you ever lost a job because your homosexuality became known?
   Yes, more than once 1
   Yes, once 2
   No 3

5. Have there been problems on any job you've had because people suspected or knew you were homosexual?
   No 1

Yes, but only to a very
   small degree 2
   Yes, to some degree 3
   Yes, very much so 4

6. How many moves have you made from one town or city to another since you were 18? (Please do not include moves made in connection with your military service.)

7. How long have you lived in the Metropolitan/Bay area?
   For less than 6 months 1
   For less than a year 2
   From 1 to 4 years 3
   From 5 to 10 years 4
   Over 10 years 5

8. How long do you expect to stay in the Metropolitan/Bay area?
   Less than a year 1
   From 1 to 2 years 2
   From 3 to 4 years 3
   From 5 to 10 years 4
   Over 10 years 5

9. Of the following people, check how many suspect or know that you are homosexual.

	All	Most	More than Half	Half	Less than Half	Few	None
Heterosexuals you know							
Male heterosexual friends							
Female heterosexual friends ..							
Aunts and uncles							
Other relatives							
Neighbors							
Work associates							
People whom *you* suspect or know are homosexual							

10. Do any of the following know or suspect that you are homosexual?

	Definitely Knows	Definitely or Probably Suspects	Do(es) Not Seem to Know or Suspect
Your mother			
Your father			
Brother(s)			
Sister(s)			
Best heterosexual friend of same sex			
Wife			
Best heterosexual friend of opposite sex			
Your employer			

11. How many people you work-(ed) with know (knew) about your homosexuality in your current (or last full-time) job?

    All 1
    Most 2
    Some 3
    Few 4
    None 5
    Don't know 6

12. Even though it may be difficult, please specify the exact number of people whom you consider to be your *close* friends. (e.g., 0, 1, 2, 3, 4 ....)

13. Of these close friends, write the number that are homosexual.

14. How important is it to you that each of the following has a good opinion of you?

	Very Important	Somewhat Important	Not Very Important	Not at all Important
Heterosexuals in general	_____	_____	_____	_____
Best homosexual friends	_____	_____	_____	_____
Homosexuals in general	_____	_____	_____	_____

15. To what extent do you care *at the present time* that certain people might find out about your homosexuality?
    Very concerned 1
    Somewhat concerned 2
    Very little concerned 3
    Not concerned at all 4

16. At the present time how extensive are your homosexual activities?
    Not active at all 1
    Not too active 2
    Somewhat active 3
    Very active 4

17. At the present time how often do you hang around with gay people?
    At least once a week 1
    About once every
      other week 2
    About once a month 3
    About once every
      2–5 months 4
    About once every
      6–12 months 5
    Less often 6
    Never 7

18. At the present time do you think of yourself as
    Exclusively homosexual ...1
    Mainly homosexual and

insignificantly
  heterosexual 2
Mainly homosexual and
  significantly
  heterosexual 3
Equally homosexual and
  heterosexual 4
Mainly heterosexual and
  significantly
  homosexual 5
Mainly heterosexual and
  insignificantly
  homosexual 6
Exclusively heterosexual ..7

19. At the present time do you have homosexual sex
    More than once a week ...1
    About once a week 2
    About once every other
      week 3
    About once a month 4
    About once every 2–5
      months 5
    About once every 6–12
      months 6
    Less often 7
    Never 8

20. How often do you go to gay bars?
    More than once a week 1
    About once a week 2
    About once every

other week 3
About once a month 4
About once every
    2–5 months 5
About once every
    6–12 months 6
Less often 7
Never 8

21. Have you ever gone in drag?
    Yes_____ No_____
    If YES, how often?
        Quite often 1
        Not very often 2
        Hardly ever 3
    Where was this? _____
    _____

    How old were you the first time
    you did this?_____
    _____

22. At the present time, what pro-
    portion of *all* your friends are
    homosexual?
        None 1
        Under 10% 2
        10–25% 3
        26–50% 4
        51–75% 5
        Over 75% 6

23. Have you ever lived with a male
    friend who was also a homo-
    sexual?
        Yes_____ No_____
    If YES, are you still living in a
    similar situation?
        Yes_____ No_____
    How long has this been the
    case? _____
    How old were you the first time
    you did this?_____

24. Have you ever been married?
    Yes_____ No_____
    (If NO, go on to question 25.)
    If YES,
    How many times? _____

How old were you the first
time? _____
Are you presently married?
    Yes_____ No_____
If YES,
Do you live with your wife?
    Yes_____ No_____
How long has your marriage
lasted? _____
Would you say you are happily
married?
    Yes_____ No_____
How many children do you
have? _____
Does your wife know you are
homosexual?
    Yes_____ No_____
How often do you have sexual
intercourse with your wife?
        6 times a week or more 1
        4–5 times a week 2
        2–3 times a week 3
        Once a week 4
        Less often 5
        Never 6
While you were married, did
you have any sexual activity
with men?
    Yes_____ No_____

25. Have you ever had sexual inter-
    course with a female?
        Yes_____ No_____
    If YES,
    How old were you the first time
    this happened? _____
    How many times in the last 6
    months have you had sexual re-
    lations with females?
    _____

    If NO,
    How many dates have you had
    with women in the last 6
    months?
    _____

Do you think you will ever get married?

Yes_____ No_____

26. Does knowing that you are homosexual "weigh on your mind" (make you feel guilty, depressed, anxious or ashamed)?

A great deal 1
Somewhat 2
Not very much 3
Not at all 4

27. At the present time do you ever experience shame, guilt, or anxiety after having homosexual relations?

Nearly always 1
Pretty often 2
Not very much 3
Never 4

28. What religion were you brought up in?

_____

What religion are you now?

_____

How important is religion to you in your life?

Very important 1
Fairly important 2
Of little importance 3
Of no importance at all ...4

29. How often do you attend church or synagogue?

More than once a week ...1
About once a week 2
About once every
    other week 3
About once a month 4
About once every
    2–5 months 5
About once every
    6–12 months 6
Not at all 7

30. How often do you vote in national and local elections?

Often 1

Sometimes 2
Rarely 3
Never 4

31. When you vote, what party do you usually vote for in national and local elections?

Republican 1
Democrat 2
Liberal 3
Conservative 4
Other (specify) 5
Don't vote 6

32. On most issues of the day, would you call yourself

Conservative 1
Moderately conservative ..2
Moderately liberal 3
Liberal 4

33. How interested are you in national politics?

Very interested 1
Somewhat interested 2
Slightly interested 3
Not interested at all 4

34. Do you have any relationship to the Mattachine Society/S.I.R.?

Yes_____ No_____

If YES, are you:

A member 1
A subscriber 2
On the mailing list only ...3

If NO, do you belong to any other homophile society?

Yes_____ No_____

35. How active are you in Mattachine/S.I.R. or any other homophile organization?

Very active 1
Fairly active 2
Not very active 3
Not active at all 4

36. How often do you go out drinking?

Every day 1
4 or more times a week ...2

1–3 times a week 3
About once every
 two weeks 4
About once a month 5
Less than once a month ...6
Never 7

37. Would you classify yourself as
 A nondrinker 1
 An occasional drinker 2
 A moderate drinker 3
 A heavy drinker 4

38. How often in the last year have
 you drunk enough so that you
 felt high?
 More than twice a week ..1
 About once a week 2
 2–3 times a month 3
 About once a month 4
 Only on special occasions ..5
 Less often 6
 Never 7

39. Have you ever regularly used
 sleeping pills, pep pills, or
 tranquilizers?
 Yes_____ No_____
 If YES,
 How old were you the first time
 you began regularly to do this?
 _____
 Do you still regularly use any
 of them?
 Yes_____ No_____

40. Have you ever seriously con-

sidered suicide?
 Yes_____ No_____
 If YES,
 How many times? _____
 How old were you the
 first time? _____
 Have you ever attempted
 suicide?
 Yes_____ No_____
 If YES,
 How old were you the first time
 you did this? _____
 How long ago was your most
 recent attempt? _____
 Had any of these attempts any-
 thing to do with homosexuality?
 Yes_____ No_____

41. Do you ever feel confused?
 Never 1
 Seldom 2
 Often 3
 Very often 4

42. Do you feel lonely?
 Never 1
 Seldom 2
 Often 3
 Very often 4

43. On the whole, how happy
 would you say you are?
 Very happy 1
 Fairly happy 2
 Not very happy 3
 Very unhappy 4

WOULD YOU AGREE OR DISAGREE WITH THE
FOLLOWING STATEMENTS:

44. I feel that I don't have enough
 friends.
 Strongly agree 1
 Agree 2
 Disagree 3
 Strongly disagree 4

45. I wish I could have more respect for myself.
 Strongly agree 1

 Agree 2
 Disagree 3
 Strongly disagree 4

46. I get a lot of fun out of life.
 Strongly agree 1
 Agree 2
 Disagree 3
 Strongly disagree 4

47. How often do the following things happen to you?

	Nearly all the time	Pretty often	Not very much	Never
Do you ever have any trouble getting to sleep or staying asleep?				
Have you ever been bothered by nervousness, feeling fidgety and tense?				
Are you ever troubled by headaches or pains in the head?				
Do you have loss of appetite?				
How often are you bothered by having an upset stomach?				
Do you find it difficult to get up in the morning?				
Have you ever been bothered by shortness of breath when you were not exercising or working hard?				
Have you ever been bothered by your heart beating hard?				
Do you ever drink more than you should?				
Have you ever had spells of dizziness?				
Are you ever bothered by nightmares?				
Do you tend to lose weight when you have something important bothering you?				
Do your hands ever tremble enough to bother you?				
Are you troubled by your hands sweating so that you feel damp and clammy?				
Have there ever been times when you couldn't take care of things because you just couldn't get going?				

BIBLIOGRAPHY

BIBLIOGRAPHY

Achilles, Nancy. "The Development of the Homosexual Bar as an Institution." *Sexual Deviance.* Edited by John H. Gagnon and William Simon. New York: Harper & Row, 1967.

Anon. "How Faked Faggotry Can Lead to Your Honorable Discharge." *The Realist,* 76 (January 1968), 11–12, 14.

Becker, Howard S. *Outsiders: Studies in the Sociology of Deviance.* New York: Free Press, 1964.

Bednar, Richard J. "Discharge and Dismissal as Punishments in the Armed Services." *Military Law Review,* DA Pam. 27–100–16 (April 1, 1962), 1–42.

Bieber, Irving, et al. *Homosexuality: A Psychoanalytic Study.* New York: Basic Books, 1961.

Bonjean, Charles M., and McGee, Reece. "Scholastic Dishonesty Among Undergraduates in Differing Systems of Control." *Sociology of Education,* 38 (Winter 1965), 127–37.

Bordua, David. "Recent Trends: Deviant Behavior and Social Control." *Annals of the American Academy of Political and Social Science,* 369 (January 1967), 149–63.

Chambliss, William J., and Liell, John T. "The Legal Process in the Community Setting." *Crime and Delinquency,* 12 (October 1966), 310–17.

Cicourel, Aaron V. *Method and Measurement in Sociology.* New York: Free Press, 1964.

Cooley, Charles H. *Human Nature and the Social Order.* New York: Scribner's, 1902.

Creech, William A. "Congress Looks to the Serviceman's Rights." *American Bar Association Journal,* Vol. 49, No. 11 (1963), 1070–74.

Daniels, Arlene K. "The Social Construction of Military Psychiatric Diagnoses." *Recent Sociology No. 2: Patterns of Communicative Behavior.* Edited by Hans Peter Dreitzel. New York: Macmillan, 1970.

Dougherty, Clifford A., and Lynch, Norman B. "Administrative Discharge: Loophole in Military Justice?" *Trial,* 4 (February–March 1968), 19–21.

———, and Lynch, Norman B. "The Administrative Discharge: Military Justice?" *George Washington Law Review,* Vol. 33, No. 2 (1964), 498–528.

Druss, Richard G. "Cases of Suspected Homosexuality Seen at an Army Mental Hygiene Consultation Service." *Psychiatric Quarterly,* 41 (January 1967), 62–70.

Edgerton, Robert B. *The Cloak of Competence: Stigma in the Lives of the Mentally Retarded.* Berkeley and Los Angeles: University of California Press, 1967.

Ehrmann, Winston. *Pre-marital Dating Behavior.* New York: Holt, 1959.

Elkin, Henry. "Aggressive and Erotic Tendencies in Army Life." *American Journal of Sociology,* 51 (March 1946), 408–13.

Etzioni, Amitai. *A Comparative Analysis of Complex Organizations.* New York: Free Press, 1961.

Everhard, John A. "Problems Involving the Disposition of Homosexuals in the Service." *Air Force Judge Advocate General's Bulletin,* II, No. 6 (1960), 20–23.

Freeman, Linton C. *Elementary Applied Statistics: For Students in Behavioral Science.* New York: Wiley, 1965.

Fry, C. C., and Rostow, E. G. *National Research Council,* interim report OEM, Cmr. 337, April 1, 1945.

Garfinkel, Harold. "Passing and the Managed Achievement of Sex Status in an Intersexed Person." *Studies in Ethnomethodology.* Englewood Cliffs, N.J.: Prentice-Hall, 1967.

Gibbs, Jack. "Conceptions of Deviant Behavior: The Old and the New." *Pacific Sociological Review,* Vol. 9, No. 1 (Spring 1966), 9–14.

Glaser, Daniel. *The Effectiveness of a Prison and Parole System.* Indianapolis: Bobbs-Merrill, 1964.

Goffman, Erving. *Asylums: Essays on the Social Situation of Mental Patients and Other Inmates.* Garden City, N.Y.: Doubleday, Anchor Books, 1961.

———. *Stigma: Notes on the Management of Spoiled Identity.* Englewood Cliffs, N.J.: Prentice-Hall, 1965.

Goodman, Leo. "Simple Methods for Analyzing Three Factor Interaction in Contingency Tables." *Journal of the American Statistical Association,* 59 (June 1964), 319–52.

Gordon, Chad. "Self Conceptions: Configurations of Content." *The Self in Social Interaction.* Edited by Chad Gordon and Kenneth J. Gergen. New York: Wiley, 1968.

Gouldner, Alvin W. "The Sociologist as Partisan: Sociology and the Welfare State." *American Sociologist,* 3 (May 1968), 103–16.

Hirschi, Travis, and Selvin, Hannan C. *Delinquency Research: An Appraisal of Analytic Methods.* New York: Free Press, 1967.

Hooker, Evelyn. "The Homosexual Community." *Perspectives in Psychopathology.* Edited by James O. Palmer and Michael J. Goldstein. New York: Oxford University Press, 1966.

Janis, Irving L. "Psychodynamic Aspects of Adjustment to Army Life." *Psychiatry,* 8 (May 1945), 159–76.

Kinsey, Alfred C., Pomeroy, Wardell B., and Martin, Clyde E. *Sexual Behavior in the Human Male.* Philadelphia: Saunders, 1948.

Kitsuse, John I. "Societal Reactions to Deviant Behavior: Problems of Theory and Method." *Social Problems,* 9 (Winter 1962), 247–56.

Labowitz, Sandford. "Criteria for Selecting a Significance Level: A Note on the Sacredness of .05." *American Sociologist,* 3 (August 1968), 220–22.

Laing, R. D. *The Politics of Experience.* London: Penguin Books, 1967.
Lemert, Edwin M. *Human Deviance: Social Problems and Social Control.* Englewood Cliffs, N.J.: Prentice-Hall, 1967.
———. *Social Pathology.* New York: McGraw-Hill, 1951.
Loesser, Lewis H. "The Sexual Psychopath in the Military Service: A Study of 270 Cases." *American Journal of Psychiatry,* 102 (July 1945), 92–101.
Lorber, Judith. "Deviance as Performance: The Case of Illness." *Social Problems,* 14 (Winter 1967), 302–10.
Lynch, Norman B. "The Administrative Discharge: Changes Needed?" *Maine Law Review,* 22 (1970), 141–69.
Matza, David. *Delinquency and Drift.* New York: Wiley, 1964.
Menninger, William C. *Psychiatry in a Troubled World: Yesterday's War and Today's Challenge.* New York: Macmillan, 1948.
Reiss, Albert J. "The Social Integration of Queers and Peers." *Social Problems,* 9 (Fall 1961), 102–20.
Riley, Matilda White. *Sociological Research.* New York: Harcourt, Brace & World, 1963.
Rosenberg, Morris. *Society and the Adolescent Self Image.* Princeton, N.J.: Princeton University Press, 1965.
Rubington, Earl, and Weinberg, Martin S. *Deviance: The Interactionist Perspective.* New York: Macmillan, 1968.
Sagarin, Edward. *Structure and Ideology in an Association of Deviants.* Unpublished Ph.D. dissertation, New York University, 1966.
Sanford, David. "Boxed In." *New Republic,* 154 (May 21, 1966), 8–9.
Scheff, Thomas J. "The Societal Reaction to Deviance: Ascriptive Elements in the Psychiatric Screening of Mental Patients in a Midwestern State." *Social Problems,* 11 (Spring 1964), 401–13.
———. "Typification in the Diagnostic Practices of Rehabilitation Agencies." *Sociology and Rehabilitation.* Edited by Marvin B. Sussman. Cleveland: American Sociological Association, 1966.
Schur, Edwin M. *Crimes Without Victims.* Englewood Cliffs, N.J.: Prentice-Hall, 1965.
Schutz, Alfred. *Collected Papers.* I: *The Problem of Social Reality.* Edited by Maurice Natenson. The Hague: Martinus Nijhoff, 1962.
———. *Collected Papers.* II: *Studies in Social Theory.* Edited by Arvid Brodersen. The Hague: Martinus Nijhoff, 1964.
Scott, Marvin B., and Lyman, Stanford M. "Paranoia, Homosexuality and Game Theory." *Journal of Health and Social Behavior,* 9 (September 1968), 179–87.
Sheppe, William M., Jr. "The Problem of Homosexuality in the Armed Forces." *Medical Aspects of Human Sexuality* III (October 1969), 65–88.
Sherman, Edward L. "The Civilianization of Military Law." *Maine Law Review,* 22 (1970), 141–69.
Simon, William, and Gagnon, John H. "Homosexuality: The Formulation of a Sociological Perspective." *Journal of Health and Social Behavior,* 9 (September 1968), 179–87.

Skipper, James K., Guenther, Anthony L., and Nass, Gilbert. "The Sacredness of .05: A Note Concerning the Uses of Statistical Levels of Significance in Social Science." *American Sociologist,* 2 (February 1967), 16–19.

Society for Individual Rights. *The Armed Services and Homosexuality.* San Francisco: Society for Individual Rights (no date).

Sudnow, David. "Normal Crimes: Sociological Features of the Penal Code in a Public Defender's Office." *Social Problems,* 12 (Winter 1965), 255–76.

Susskind, Jerome A. "Military Administrative Discharge Boards: The Right to Confrontation and Cross Examination." *Michigan State Bar Journal,* Vol. 46, No. 1 (January 1965), 25–32.

Sykes, Gresham M., and Matza, David. "Techniques of Neutralization: A Theory of Delinquency." *American Sociological Review,* 22 (December 1957), 664–70.

United States Senate. *Constitutional Rights of Military Personnel.* Subcommittee on Constitutional Rights of the Senate Committee on the Judiciary 87th Congress, 2nd Session, 1962.

United States Senate. *Military Justice.* Subcommittee on Constitutional Rights of the Senate Committee on the Judiciary 89th Congress, 2nd Session, 1966.

United States Congress, Senate Committee on Expenditures in the Executive Departments, Subcommittee on Investigations. "Employment of Homosexuals and Other Sex Perverts in Government," 1950.

Viditch, Arthur J., and Stein, Maurice R. "The Dissolved Identity in Military Life." *Identity and Anxiety: Survival of the Person in Mass Society.* Edited by Maurice R. Stein, Arthur J. Viditch, and David Manning White. New York: Free Press, 1960.

Weinberg, Martin S. "Homosexual Samples: Differences and Similarities." *Journal of Sex Research,* 6 (November 1970), 312–25.

————, and Williams, Colin J. *The Male Homosexual: A Cross-Cultural Study in Psycho-Sociology,* in process.

West, Louis Jolyon, Doidge, William T., and Williams, R. L. "An Approach to the Problem of Homosexuality in the Military Service." *American Journal of Psychiatry,* 115 (November 1958), 392–401.

West, Louis Jolyon, and Glass, Albert J. "Sexual Behavior and the Military Law." *Sexual Behavior and the Law.* Edited by Ralph Slovenko. Springfield, Ill.: Charles C Thomas, 1965.

INDEX

INDEX

71 72 73 8 7 6 5 4 3 2 1